The Complex

Marie-Louise von Franz, Honorary Patron

**Studies in Jungian Psychology
by Jungian Analysts**

Daryl Sharp, General Editor

THE COMPLEX

Path of Transformation from Archetype to Ego

EREL SHALIT

National Library of Canada Cataloguing in Publication Data

Shalit, Erel
    The complex: path of transformation from archetype to ego

(Studies in Jungian psychology by Jungian analysts; no. 98)

Includes bibliographical references and index.

ISBN 0-919123-99-6

1. Complexes (Psychology).
2. Archetype (Psychology).
3. Psychoanalysis.
4. Jungian Psychology.
I. Title. II. Series.

BF173.S43 2002   154.2'4   C2001-901446-5

INNER CITY BOOKS
Box 1271, Station Q, Toronto, ON M4T 2P4, Canada

Telephone (416) 927-0355 / FAX (416) 924-1814
Web site: www.innercitybooks.net / E-mail: admin@innercitybooks.net

Honorary Patron: Marie-Louise von Franz.
Publisher and General Editor: Daryl Sharp.
Senior Editor: Victoria Cowan.

INNER CITY BOOKS was founded in 1980 to promote the
understanding and practical application of the work of C.G. Jung.

Illustration by Jenny Ahban

Printed and bound in Canada by University of Toronto Press Incorporated

CONTENTS

4 The Complex in the Shadow 68

Preface

At the turn of the last century, as the wheels of industrialization and scientific progress turned ever faster, Sigmund Freud provocatively insisted on the existence of an inner world of drives and instincts hidden behind our polished exterior. He insisted on the dynamics of the psyche, laying bare the sexuality squeezed in behind the girdle of the hysteric. He uncovered the dream as the "royal road to the unconscious,"[1] which Jung, his heir-turned-rival, modified by claiming instead that "the *via regia* to the unconscious . . . is not the dream . . . but the complex, which is the architect of dreams and of symptoms."[2]

From the perspective of analytical psychology it may be more appropriate to view not the complex but the central archetype of the Self as the architect of the dream. As the archetype of order and meaning *(arche* means first, *typos* means mold or pattern), the Self draws up the blueprint from which are crafted both the personality and the building blocks of the dream. Our conscious ego is not the author of the dream narrative related to us in our sleep. In the Talmud (the body of Jewish law, legend and Bible commentaries) it says that a dream not interpreted is like a letter not read. The best we can do is to read the letter and ponder its meaning(s). Besides its other tasks, such as decision making and classification, the ego needs to be an active and reflective recipient of the treasures that arise from the unconscious.

In daring contrast to many of his contemporaries, who were mainly caught up in a fascination with progress, Freud looked out over the vast lands beyond the boundaries of consciousness. Through attentive introspection he penetrated personal layers of resistance, finding what he understood to be the dream's true meaning—latent, hidden behind the overt material. He concluded that the unconscious told its true story in the subtext concealed beneath the cryptic narrative.

Jung ascribed no less significance than Freud to the unconscious. How-

---

[1] *The Interpretation of Dreams,* SE 5, p. 608. (SE refers throughout to *The Standard Edition of the Works of Sigmund Freud)*

[2] "A Review of the Complex Theory," *The Structure and Dynamics of the Psyche,* CW 8, par. 210. (CW refers throughout to *The Collected Works of C.G. Jung)*

ever, he seemed more at home in the vicinity of the unconscious—though with no less pain. As Jeffrey Satinover observes, "Freud saw an essentially psychoneurotic world, Jung an essentially 'narcissistic-neurotic' or psychotic one."[3] Others have referred to this as Jung's creative illness. He thought of the dream the other way around, as "part of nature, which harbors no intention to deceive, but expresses something as best it can, . . . but we may deceive ourselves, because our eyes are shortsighted."[4]

To Jung, it is consciousness that is short-sighted, while the unconscious is honest and healing. If we do not bring a conscious relationship to it, however, the unconscious may become chaotic, even lethal.

The complexes, then, are more like the construction workers who give visible and comprehensible shape to underlying archetypal blueprints. It is through the complexes that we manage to approach the unconscious without being overwhelmed and engulfed by it. Likewise, by means of the complexes the unconscious approaches us. In Jung's words,

> Complexes are in truth the living units of the unconscious psyche, and it is only through them that we are able to deduce its existence and its constitution.[5]

Thus, if it weren't for the complexes, the archetypes would remain empty and purely formal possibilities of representation. Jung says,

> A primordial image is determined as to its content only when it has become conscious and is therefore filled out with the material of conscious experience. Its form, however, . . . might perhaps be compared to the axial system of a crystal, which, as it were, preforms the crystalline structure in the mother liquid, although it has no material existence of its own. . . . The archetype in itself is empty and purely formal, nothing but a *facultas praeformandi*, a possibility of representation which is given *a priori*.[6]

In other words, the complex serves as the vehicle that fleshes out the archetype, giving it human shape and personal body.

My intention in this book is to clarify the purposeful, teleological es-

---

[3] "Jung's Lost Contribution to the Dilemma of Narcissism," in *Journal of the American Psychoanalytic Association*, vol. 34 (1986), p. 411.

[4] *Memories, Dreams, Reflections*, pp. 161f.

[5] "A Review of the Complex Theory," *The Structure and Dynamics of the Psyche*, CW 8, par. 210.

[6] "Psychological Aspects of the Mother Archetype," *The Archetypes and the Collective Unconscious*, CW 9i, par. 155.

sence of complexes, as well as their pathological, shadowy manifestations, and to show how an autonomous complex, dissociated from one's conscious identity, comes to thrive and gather strength in the shadow. An autonomous complex competes with the ego for available psychic energy. As Jung so pertinently says, the *via regia* to the unconscious is not so very royal, but rather "more like a rough and uncommonly devious footpath that often loses itself in the undergrowth."[7]

The Oedipus complex, so central to Freudian psychoanalysis and so ambivalently related to by many Jungians, will be examined here from a Jungian perspective. Young Oedipus, incestuous and murderous, is driven by the basic life energies, Eros and Mars. While these provide the essential fuel for the complex, Oedipus' drivenness makes him the archetypal, eternal carrier of the complex that bears his name.

In the last part of this book, the autonomous complex will be considered in its capacity as pathological shadow, and some central complexes will be illustrated by means of clinical and other material.

---

[7] "A Review of the Complex Theory," *The Structure and Dynamics of the Psyche,* CW 8, par. 210.

1
The Complex in the History of Psychoanalysis

Introduction

The first use of the term complex is usually ascribed to Jung, who from 1904 onward developed his ideas by means of the Word Association Test. The British scientist Sir Francis Galton (1822-1911),[8] a cousin of Charles Darwin, had conceived the initial, elementary association experiments. Wilhelm Wundt (1832-1920), the founder of scientific psychology, who established the first laboratory for experimental psychology in 1879, further developed the association experiments systematically.

The method of the Association Test, as Jung notes, is quite simple:

> The experimenter calls out a word to the subject, who then says what is immediately called to mind by the stimulus-word. We introduce an image to the consciousness of the subject, and are given whatever further image is brought by this to his mind. We can thus quickly obtain a large number of connected images or associations.[9]

Theodor Ziehen (1862-1950) found that the reaction time between the stimulus word and the subject's response was longer when the stimulus word was related to something unpleasant to the subject.[10] Prolonged reaction times could sometimes be related to what he called a "common underlying representation," that is, an emotionally charged complex, which was found to interfere with the smooth operation of consciousness.

---

[8] Galton is considered to be the founder of eugenics, a science of selective breeding to improve the human population. Several states and countries passed sterilization laws to eliminate childbearing of, for instance, the mentally retarded, and eugenics was applied by the Nazis to justify their extermination policy. In *Mein Kampf*, Hitler writes, "Anyone who wants to cure this era, which is inwardly sick and rotten, must first of all summon up the courage to make clear the causes of this disease." (p. 435) What Hitler meant by "cause" and "cure" is evident. While subsequently falling into ill repute, eugenics might yet reappear, following a new emphasis on genetic medicine.

[9] "The Psychopathological Significance of the Association Experiment," *Experimental Researches,* CW 2, par. 868.

[10] Henri F. Ellenberger, *The Discovery of the Unconscious,* p. 692.

Jean Charcot (1825-1893) had spoken of how associated ideas could settle in the mind like parasites, isolated and cut off from conscious control.[11] Consequently, Pierre Janet (1859-1947) developed the concept of split-off personality fragments that he called "subconscious fixed ideas." Jung had attended Janet's lectures on theoretical psychopathology in 1902-1903, and equated his own conception of the complex with Janet's,[12] as well as with the propositions of Ziehen.

In fact, Freud and Josef Breuer (1842-1925) had used the term complex prior to Jung. They too followed Janet (whose critical contribution seems in fact to have somewhat complexed some of the early psychoanalysts).[13] In *Studies on Hysteria* (1895), Freud writes,

> For the most part the sense impressions that are not apperceived and the ideas that are *aroused but do not enter consciousness* cease without producing further consequences. Sometimes, however, they accumulate and form complexes—mental strata *withdrawn from consciousness*, they form a subconsciousness.[14]

Complexes that are "aroused but do not enter consciousness" have not fallen out of consciousness, but rather have never reached it. This means that complexes may constellate not solely due to repression by consciousness, but originally emerge from the unconscious, trying to knock on the door of the ego (primal repression). This is what gives the complexes their purposeful, teleological character, as shall be detailed later.

When withdrawn from and accumulating outside consciousness, as Freud and Breuer remark, the complexes come to produce further consequences. That is, when they are autonomous, outside the realm of the ego, thriving in the shadow, complexes have a drive of their own, subtracting energy from consciousness. As Breuer writes about the hysterical type,

---

[11] Ibid., p. 149.

[12] While frequently referring to and giving credit to Janet, Jung might have had something of a "Janet complex." In a letter to Freud, Jung writes that Janet "is stuck in his groove and is, be it said in passing, merely an intellectual but not a personality, a hollow *causeur* and a typical mediocre bourgeois" *(The Freud/Jung Letters,* pp. 65f.) , and elsewhere: "A ghastly crowd, reeking of vanity, Janet the worst of the lot." (Ibid., p. 83)

[13] Ernest Jones, ever loyal to Freud, asserts that "Freud's discoveries owed nothing to Janet." (Ellenberger, *The Discovery of the Unconscious,* p. 408)

[14] SE 2, p. 231 (italics added).

It is not the case that the splitting of consciousness occurs because the patients are weak-minded; they appear to be weak-minded because their mental activity is divided and only a part of its capacity is at the disposal of their conscious thought.[15]

These early formulations of Freud and Breuer's are surprisingly similar to Jung's conception, for instance when he speaks of complexes as "psychic fragments which have split off":

They produce disturbances of memory and blockages in the flow of association; they appear and disappear according to their own laws; they can temporarily obsess consciousness . . . . In a word, complexes behave like independent beings.[16]

In "On the History of the Psychoanalytic Movement," Freud credits the Zurich school of psychoanalysis (Bleuler, and specifically Jung) with the term complex, perhaps, paradoxically, because by that time (1914) he already wished to dissociate himself from the concept. He says he does not value the contribution "so highly as others do," since, he claims,

The theory of "complexes" which grew out of the *Studies in Word-Association* (1906) . . . has neither . . . produced a psychological theory, nor has it proved capable of easy incorporation into the context of psychoanalytic theory. The word "complex" on the other hand, has become naturalized, so to speak, in psychoanalytic language; it is a convenient and often indispensable term for summing up a psychological state descriptively.[17]

Freud did initially find the concept useful, speaking for instance about his own personal, professional and family complexes.[18] In 1907 Freud playfully writes to Jung, "I should have been very sorry if your Vienna complex had been obliged to share the available cathexis with a Paris complex."[19] Freud had been concerned that Jung would be too impressed by Charcot in Paris, but Jung had assured him that "these people are 50 years behind the times."[20] Freud can remain calm, having "emerged safe

---

[15] Ibid., p. 231.
[16] "Psychological Factors in Human Behavior," *The Structure and Dynamics of the Psyche,* CW 8, par. 253.
[17] SE 14, p. 29.
[18] *The Psychopathology of Everyday Life,* SE 6, chap. 3, esp. pp. 22ff.
[19] William McGuire, ed., *The Freud/Jung Letters,* p. 68.
[20] Ibid., p. 67.

and sound from a first danger," namely the threat that Jung's interest in Janet's Paris school might have detracted his (Jung's) energy from "the new life of psychiatry . . . between Zürich and Vienna."[21]

When writing up the case of the Rat Man (1909),[22] Freud was still on good terms with Jung, and spoke of "repressed complexes" and "complex sensitivity," and, as John Kerr writes,

> At one point, he even had some fun with this game of making the crew from Zurich comfortable; Freud described the scene in which his patient first heard of using rats to torture people thus:
>
> "It was almost as though Fate, when the captain told him his story, had been putting him through an association-test; she had called out a 'complex stimulus-word,' and he had reacted to it with his obsessional idea.' "[23]

While Freud had initially welcomed Jung's association experiments, seeing them and the formulation of complexes as scientific evidence of the validity of psychoanalysis, he eventually became critical. He writes:

> Analysts began to speak among themselves of a "return of a complex" where they meant a "return of the repressed," or fell into the habit of saying "I have a complex against him" where the only correct expression would have been "a resistance against him."[24]

The complex has largely lost its importance in Freudian thinking. It has sunk into psychoanalysis's ill-reputed Jungian shadow. Nowadays, it is practically only used for that—though very central—idea, the Oedipus complex, and the castration complex (which is usually thought of as integrated into the Oedipus complex, manifested in his blinding).

---

[21] Ibid., p. 68. That is, Freud acts in a way typical of a father with a son complex, who fears any upcoming new element, similar to, though less violent than Laius, father of Oedipus (see below, pp. 44ff.). Jung relates *father and son* not only to an interpersonal dynamic, but also to the intrapsychic polarity of *discipline and instinct (Symbols of Transformation,* CW 5, par. 396). The more strongly the father, as actual person or as psychic faculty, relies on discipline, the less room is there for the son's instinctuality. Likewise, a controlling ego and a rigid identity do not permit new complexes that rise from the shadow to enter into consciousness. However, as regards their mutual relationship, Jung temporarily remained a disciplined son of Freud's, reining in his instinctual rebelliousness.

[22] "Notes Upon a Case of Obsessional Neurosis," SE 10.

[23] *A Most Dangerous Method,* p. 185; ibid., p. 216.

[24] *On the History of the Psycho-Analytic Movement,* SE 14, p. 30.

In Freud's search for verity, the Oedipus complex became the core or nuclear complex, underlying both neurotic symptom and mythical drama. Freud says at the end of the analysis of Little Hans (1909), that in spite of "the multiplicity of the phenomena of repression exhibited by neuroses and the abundance of their pathogenic material," they might be derived "from a very limited number of processes concerned with identical ideational complexes."[25]

A Plenitude of Complexes

In contrast to the Freudian view, according to which Oedipus delineates *the* one central complex, Jungian psychology is full of complexes. In a letter to Sándor Ferenczi (1873-1933), Freud writes that there is a Jungian "complex-mythology."[26] In fact, if we accept Jung's idea of the archetype as "a possibility of representation," then the archetypes can coalesce and unfold in an infinite number of possible representations. Since complexes develop around an archetypal core, any number of complexes can, consequently, be defined and described. Hans Dieckmann observes that "the number of possible complexes . . . corresponds to the number of inherent archetypes," and considers the number to be "incredibly high" but "not infinite."[27] He thereby follows Jung, who claims that "the complexes are not infinitely variable."[28]

From a Jungian perspective the unconscious is vast and boundaryless, while consciousness is by definition rationed, limited in scope, "shortsighted." We might therefore be capable of perceiving and formulating only a limited number of archetypal representations and complexes, which in themselves may combine beyond the scope of our imagination. Jung must have been somewhat ambivalent on the subject, since in "A Psychological Theory of Types" (1931) he states that "complexes are infinitely varied, yet careful comparison reveals a relatively small number of typical primary forms."[29]

Even if theoretically an infinity of complexes may constellate, we may discern some central complexes of everyday life. Among these are father

---

[25] "Analysis of a Phobia in a Five-Year-Old Boy," SE 10, p. 147.

[26] Ernest Jones, *Sigmund Freud: Life and Work,* p. 188.

[27] *Complexes:Diagnosis and Therapy in Analytical Psychology,* p. 2.

[28] Jolande Jacobi, *Complex/Archetype/Symbol,* foreword, p. ix.

[29] *Psychological Types,* CW 6, par. 927.

and mother complexes, brother and sister complexes, anger, incest, power and death complexes.

The so-called superiority and inferiority complexes originate with Alfred Adler (1870-1937).[30] The wish for superiority is compensatory to feelings of inferiority. Adler formulated a general concept, "that all men are inferior and weak at birth and thus begin a lifelong struggle to elevate themselves from their present levels."[31] Thus his conception is founded on the image of a ladder that one climbs. Adler saw this process as an archetypal one, as for instance echoed in his belief that "wanting to be superior is a universal and timeless property of man's personality."[32]

If we turn to Greek mythology, we find an image of the archetypal core of the superiority complex in *hubris*, the desire to be like or to dethrone the gods. This reflects an ego that strives to incorporate *mana,* archetypal energy, without recognizing its limitations. Such an ego desires to be god-like and complex-free.

We find an image of the core of the inferiority complex in Nemesis, goddess of measurement and retribution for good fortune, who reminds the ego of its minuteness and its boundaries. Jung says of the inferiority complex that it

> surely plays a very great role, almost just as great as the sex complex. You see, the sex complex belongs to a hedonistic type of man who thinks in terms of his pleasure and displeasure, while there is another class of man, chiefly the man who has not arrived, who thinks in terms of power and defeat, and to him it is far more important to win out somewhere than his whole sex problem.[33]

The person who suffers from an inferiority complex "has not arrived" yet, and feels defeated before setting out. In fact, the inferiority complex may withhold from the ego even the necessary minimum of adequate (primary) narcissistic energy, thus preventing the person from even departing on his or her journey.

---

[30] These principles do not correspond to the superior and inferior functions in Jung's model of typology, which relate to the structure of consciousness but not its content; any of the four functions may be superior, auxiliary or inferior.

[31] Ledford J. Bischof, *Interpreting Personality Theories,* p. 236.

[32] Ibid., p. 237.

[33] "The Stephen Black Interviews," in William McGuire and R.F.C. Hull, *C.G. Jung Speaking,* p. 257.

The plenitude of complexes in Jungian psychology reflects its "polytheistic" aspect, or the "polycentric psyche."[34] In his doctoral dissertation, "On the Psychology and Pathology of So-called Occult Phenomena" (1902), where he reports on the seances with his maternal cousin, Helen Preiswerk, Jung already discusses "the disaggregation of psychic complexes."[35] In his study of this young and problematic relative, Jung was able to observe the independent operation and personification of complexes,[36] and the divisibility of the psyche. He concludes,

> The psyche is not an indivisible unity but a divisible and more or less divided whole. Although the separate parts are connected with one another, they are relatively independent, so much so that certain parts of the psyche never become associated with the ego at all, or only very rarely. I have called these psychic fragments "autonomous complexes," and I based my theory of complexes on their existence.[37]

That is, in contrast to Freud's core complex, the complexes in analytical psychology populate the soul's universe, primarily not in conflict with the ego complex but aimed, rather, at enabling its dynamism and vitality.

Jung's Personal Complexes

As has repeatedly been stated, psychological theories inevitably reflect the psychology of their originators. We can benefit from the disclosure that Jung himself took the Word Association Experiment in 1907. The results revealed eleven major complexes at work in Jung at the time.[38] The most significant were a repentance complex, a death-of-father complex, a wish-for-a-son complex, and a conspicuous Goethe complex.

The repentance complex disclosed Jung's feelings and attitudes toward his love affair with Sabina Spielrein, his first psychoanalytic patient.[39] Binswanger, who conducted the test, was careful not to analyze it, "for

---

[34] Andrew Samuels, *Jung and the Post-Jungians*, p. 117.

[35] *Psychiatric Studies*, CW 1, par. 93.

[36] See *Memories, Dreams, Reflections*, p. 322.

[37] "The Psychological Foundations of Belief in Spirits," *The Structure and Dynamics of the Psyche*, CW 8, par. 582.

[38] William McGuire, "Jung's Complex Reactions (1907): Word Association Experiments Performed by Binswanger," p. 18.

[39] See Aldo Carotenuto, *A Secret Symmetry: Sabina Spielrein between Jung and Freud*, pp. 153ff; also John Kerr, *A Most Dangerous Method*, pp. 66f.

personal reasons,"[40] since there was "the great embarrassment of the subject at revealing this complex."[41] In fact, when Jung rested at the end of the experiment he fell asleep and "had a dream in which this lady played the chief part."[42] Binswanger refers, perhaps condescendingly, to this as an "unpleasant complex."[43]

Jung's wish-for-a-son complex was arguably acted out in his countertransference toward Sabina Spielrein. We should be careful, however, when passing judgment. The very idea of the countertransference had not yet been conceived. Freud may in fact have formulated it in light of Jung's reactions to Sabina Spielrein. Jung seems not to have fully recognized that her desire to bear him a son was to be understood transferentially and symbolically, and he might to some extent have taken it literally. Spielrein was obsessed by her thoughts and feelings about the fantasy child, and certainly tried to seduce Jung into her fantasy world, for instance writing him (in 1912), "Receive now the product of our love, the project which is your little son Siegfrid."[44]

Yet, at least at a later stage, she does seem to have grasped the transference and its symbolic aspect, as when she writes to Jung (in 1918), asking, "What did my youthful Siegfrid symbolism signify if it could not be taken literally?"[45] Spielrein recognizes that Siegfrid had been real for her subconscious, "which cleverly saw through your own [Jung's] subconscious attitude."[46] Her emphasis on the symbolic aspect is evident when she writes, in another letter to Jung soon afterward (also in January 1918):

> Without your instruction I would have believed . . . that I was dreaming of Siegfrid, since I am always dwelling on heroic fantasies. . . . I am, and most especially always was, somewhat mystical in my leanings; I violently resisted the interpretation of Siegfrid as a real child.[47]

She also, importantly, notices how energy compounds and stiffens in complexes, and is released by the progression of libido, for instance by

---

[40] McGuire, "Jung's Complex Reactions," p. 4.
[41] Ibid., p. 23.
[42] Ibid., p. 31.
[43] Ibid.
[44] Carotenuto, *A Secret Symmetry,* p. 48.
[45] Ibid., p. 73.
[46] Ibid., p. 77.
[47] Ibid., pp. 79f.

means of symbolization. She writes,

> The "real" Siegfrid complex therefore had to be drained of its energy and in order to keep this energy alive, it had to be channelled into another task, that of the "Siegfrid" in sublimated form. . . . Perhaps my many dreams with sun symbolism are—Siegfrid dreams?[48]

That is, the "real Siegfrid" complex was sacrificed by conscious processing and thus sublimated. In fact, we might understand her desire to bear Jung a child as the culmination of her Oedipal father-transference.

Jung himself was well aware of his father complex. In "A Rejoinder to Dr. Bally," he says, "I also admit to my so-called 'father complex': I do not want to knuckle under to any 'fathers' and never shall."[49] As has often been observed, Jung's relationship to his father was ambivalent.[50] To Jung, "father" meant "reliability and—powerlessness."[51] He had "profound doubts about everything my father said," which sounded "stale and hollow, like a tale told by someone who . . . cannot quite believe it himself."[52] Indeed, Jung's autobiography is scattered with judgmental statements and belittlement of his father, who bored and disappointed him. Joel Ryce-Menuhin tries to correct the complex-ridden picture of Jung's father, Paul Achilles Jung, saying that the elder Jung

> proves himself to be a true monotheist with a much broader range of comprehension of the sources of the Semitic religions than Jungians have realized. . . . Jung's repeatedly disappointed remarks about his father, for example, in the autobiography, need to be taken with a grain of salt by contemporary Jungians. Sons often do not appreciate the gifts of their fathers and lack compassion in their description of their fathers.[53]

Jung's negative father complex was acted out vis-à-vis Freud, as both

---

[48] Ibid., p. 77.

[49] This in itself is problematic, written by Jung in 1934, in defence of his "a-political" position vis-à-vis National Socialism and being "incautious" in the timing of discussing "the difference between Jewish and 'Aryan-Germanic-Christian-European' psychology." (*Civilization in Transition,* CW 10, pars. 1023ff.

[50] See, for instance, Danielle Knafo, "The Significance of the Oedipal in Dreams of Freud and Jung," p. 354.

[51] *Memories, Dreams, Reflections,* p. 8.

[52] Ibid., pp. 42f.

[53] *Jung and the Monotheisms,* p. 240.

Jung's wife and his son observed.[54] Freud himself was caught in the role of father in a son complex that inevitably would lead to anger and disillusion with his "beloved son," as he had called Jung.[55] Emma Jung wrote Freud asking him not to relate to Jung with a father's feelings of "He will grow, but I must dwindle," but rather relate to him as one human being to another, "who like you has his own law to fulfil."[56] However, Jung was caught in his own father complex, ambivalent in his role as the son, which inevitably would lead to revolt and separation. While in 1908 he begs Freud to "let me enjoy your friendship not as one between equals but as that of father and son,"[57] in 1913 he writes to Sabina Spielrein about his relationship to Freud, saying,

> I want to be a friend on an equal footing, while he wants to have me as a son. For that reason he ascribes to a complex everything I do that does not fit the framework of his life.[58]

Freud, as is well known, fainted twice in Jung's presence, suspicious of Jung's death wishes against him. He may not have been too wrong, considering Jung's contempt for his father and his projection onto Freud. Foreseeing their break, Jung dreamed of Freud as "the ghost of a customs official who had died years ago."[59] If anything, autonomous complexes are like ghosts, with an uncanny tendency to remind us of their existence years after we believe they are dead. It is the middle-aged woman who wakes up at night, looks herself in the mirror, only to see the face of her deceased and detested mother. As Jung notes, "where the primitive speaks of ghosts, the European speaks of dreams and fantasies and neurotic symptoms."[60]

---

[54] See Linda Donn, *Freud and Jung: Years of Friendship, Years of Loss*, pp. 98, 138.

[55] Paul Roazen has observed that unlike his success with "adopted daughters," Freud had trouble with all his "sons" in psychoanalysis. (*Freud And His Followers*, p. 415) We witness a similar fate of Oedipus', when no longer carrying the complex of youth but the yoke of the father, cursing his sons/brothers, who killed each other in strife over the throne, while leaning on his daughters/sisters.

[56] McGuire, *Freud/Jung Letters*, p. 457.

[57] Ibid., p. 122.

[58] Carotenuto, *A Secret Symmetry*, p. 184.

[59] *Memories, Dreams, Reflections*, p. 163.

[60] "The Psychological Foundations of Belief in Spirits," *The Structure and Dynamics of the Psyche*, CW 8, par. 573.

Beyond the mutual acting out of their respective father and son complexes, Jung identified, as well, their different approaches as regards the father versus the mother. Jung writes:

> The motif of the Gnostic Yahweh and Creator-God reappeared in the Freudian myth of the primal father and the gloomy superego deriving from that father. In Freud's myth he became a daemon who created a world of disappointments, illusions, and suffering. But the materialistic trend which had already come to light in the alchemists' preoccupation with the secrets of matter had the effect of obscuring for Freud that other essential aspect of Gnosticism: the primordial image of the spirit as another, higher god who gave to mankind the *krater* (mixing vessel), the vessel of spiritual transformation. The *krater* is a feminine principle which could find no place in Freud's patriarchal world.[61]

Jung freed himself by slaying the image of the father-daemon, the father spirit, who creates disappointment and suffering. Jung was of course keenly aware that the father, in his capacity as spirit of consciousness, brings pain and suffering. However, patricide, the slaying of the father, was imperative for Jung to freely and creatively outline his own theory, in which he turned incestuously to the realm of the Great Mother, whose womb gives birth to the symbols of transformation. Even in his greatly controversial "Answer to Job," Jung takes the Great Father to task, teaching him about human consciousness.[62]

No less interesting than his father complex was Jung's Goethe complex, which Binswanger termed "an extremely powerful complex for this subject, into which . . . we are, unfortunately, unable to enter further."[63] Jung was undoubtedly greatly influenced by Goethe's *Faust*, which served as a lifelong source of inspiration. He seems to have been ambivalent about his "legendary kinship with Goethe," according to which his grandfather, his namesake Carl Gustav Jung, was an out-of-wedlock son of Goethe's.[64] When interviewed on his eightieth birthday, Jung claimed "circumstantial evidence that my grandfather was one of Goethe's sons,"[65] and in a letter to Freud (January 18, 1911) he writes,

---

[61] *Memories, Dreams, Reflections,* p. 201.

[62] *Psychology and Religion,* CW 11.

[63] McGuire, "Jung's Complex Reactions," p. 5.

[64] *Memories, Dreams, Reflections,* p. 35.

[65] "An Eightieth Birthday Interview," in McGuire and Hull, *C.G. Jung Speaking,*

My paper is now in the process of being copied out. . . . After seeing a performance of *Faust* yesterday, . . . I feel more confident of its value. . . . I felt sure that my respected great-grandfather [i.e., Goethe] would have given my work his placet [affirmation], the more willingly as he would have noted with a smile that the great-grandchild has continued and even extended the ancestral line of thought.[66]

Aniela Jaffé points out how Jung spoke of this legend "with a certain gratified amusement,"[67] but also how he commented on it, saying that the world was full enough of "too many fools who tell such tales of the 'unknown father.' "[68] Elsewhere Jaffé says:

ne should not ascribe too much significance to this "little great-grandfather" legend. . . . Jung's references to it are generally characterized by a playful tone. What was more important was Jung's sense of a spiritual affinity to Goethe.[69]

On the one hand, Jung's feeling for Goethe may have compounded as a complex, a concretization of the spiritual father that Jung could not find in real life, or that, perhaps because of his complex, he was reluctant to acknowledge. On the other hand, Goethe did serve as a source of Jung's inspiration for looking into the depths of the human psyche. This is a good example of the fact that complexes are not necessarily negative, which will be discussed here later.

---

p. 271.
[66] *The Freud/Jung Letters*, p. 384.
[67] *Memories, Dreams, Reflections*, p. 36n.
[68] Ibid.
[69] *C.G. Jung: Word and Image*, p. 11.

2
Complex Psychology

Introduction

The complex was so important to Jung that he considered calling his approach to the psyche "complex psychology." This followed a suggestion by his friend and collaborator Toni Wolff, to whom, he writes (in an introduction to her work published posthumously in 1959), "we owe the expression 'complex psychology' as a designation for this field of research."[70] Earlier, in 1948, Jung spoke of "this memorable day of the founding of an Institute for Complex Psychology,"[71] which was the name Toni Wolff wanted for the institute.[72]

The description of Jung's approach as "complex psychology" refers, or referred, to a theoretical point of view rather than clinical practice. As Toni Wolff says:

> Nowadays Jung mostly uses the term "Complex Psychology," especially when he speaks about his psychology from a theoretical point of view. The designation "Analytical Psychology" is applicable, when we are concerned with the practice of psychological analysis.[73]

Freud stipulated Oedipus as the one core complex at the crossroads of the child's development, the grand riddle to be resolved in order to mature and pursue life's journey of love and work. In the Freudian school, other complexes have been laid to rest, buried, but still they thrive and flourish—in the shadow. And so we must ask, how come complexes are not only frequent, but even seem necessary in Jungian psychology? The answer is that the complex makes Jungian psychology into a personal psychology, not just a "mythosophical" theory of archetypes.

Most schools of psychology, including Jungian, base their theoretical understanding of a person's development to some extent on the framework of personal childhood and actual life experiences. The very conception of

---

[70] "Introduction to Toni Wolff's 'Studies in Jungian Psychology,' " *Civilization in Transition,* CW 10, par. 887.

[71] "Address on the Occasion of the Founding of the C.G. Jung Institute, Zürich, 24 April, 1948," *The Symbolic Life,* CW 18, par. 1129.

[72] Thomas Kirsch, *The Jungians: A Comparative and Historical Perspective,* p. 9.

[73] *Studien zu C.G. Jungs Psychologie,* p. 19 (author's translation).

developmental stages reflects the notion of a predetermined outline of the road that every individual comes to walk. Failure to move ahead in orderly fashion results in *dis*order. When we set out on the search for the roots and causes of psychological suffering and psychopathology, we look into the person's actual childhood experiences. While not always keenly aware of it, we keep a yardstick at hand of what childhood is typically like, what progress to expect, and what comprises deviation therefrom.

Psychodynamic and psychoanalytic theory does not, to put it mildly, accentuate its reliance on primordial possibilities of representation and universal patterns, i.e., archetypes. Although Freud did indeed have recourse to a notion he spoke of as "phylogenetic prehistory" and "phylogenetic endowment,"[74] the idea of archetypes is generally repressed into the psychoanalytic unconscious. Often, the archetypal view is supposed to negate individual freedom, as if the concept of freedom depends upon man being born a *tabula rasa*. And, strange as it may be, the opposite of the idea that man is born a clean slate is provided by modern science, obsessed with finding the gene for every behavioral and emotional manifestation. Thereby, an individual's destiny is increasingly deemed as determined by biology rather than by will and soul.

Jungian psychology, in contrast, does acknowledge and conceive of universal patterns that precede conscious experience. Already in "The Significance of the Father in the Destiny of the Individual," written in 1909, traces of Jung's evolving controversy with Freud begin to unfold

> Freud has pointed out that the emotional relationship of the child to the parents, and particularly to the father, is of a decisive significance in regard to the content of any later neurosis.[75]

He then slowly stretches the meaning of "father," asserting that "the predominating influence of the father's character in a family" often lasts "for centuries."[76] This, then, is no longer the personal father, but echoes the significance of a Biblical Father-God.[77]

---

[74] See, for instance, *Introductory Lectures on Psychoanalysis*, SE 15, p. 199; "From the History of an Infantile Neurosis," SE 17, pp. 86, 97.

[75] *Freud and Psychoanalysis*, CW 4, par. 693.

[76] Ibid., par. 695.

[77] "For I the Lord thy God am a jealous God, visiting the iniquity of the fathers upon the children to the third and fourth generation." (Ex. 20:5, AV)

Pondering back and forth, seemingly struggling with his ambivalent feelings toward Freud as his projected father, Jung says, "Freud was of the opinion that all 'divine' figures have their roots in the father-imago."[78] But, continues Jung, "we must ask ourselves whether we may attribute such magical power to an ordinary human being," whereby he reverses the order and abandons the idea that the psyche begins to take shape only after birth. He then writes:

> Man "possesses" many things which he has never acquired but has inherited from his ancestors. He is not born as a *tabula rasa,* he is merely born unconscious. But he brings with him systems that are organized and ready to function in a specifically human way, and these he owes to millions of years of human development. Just as the migratory and nest-building instincts of birds were never learnt or acquired individually, man brings with him at birth the ground-plan of his nature, and not only of his individual nature but of his collective nature. These inherited systems correspond to the human situations that have existed since primeval times: youth and old age, birth and death, sons and daughters, fathers and mothers, mating, and so on. Only the individual consciousness experiences these things for the first time, but not the bodily system and the unconscious. . . .
>
> I have called this congenital and pre-existent instinctual model, or pattern of behaviour, the *archetype.*[79]

In other words, Jungian psychology postulates an objective psyche, or collective unconscious, made up of forms, molds and energies that serve as blueprints for common and universal human experiences. These are the archetypes which, Jung clarifies,

> correspond in every way to the instincts, which are also determined in form only. The existence of the instincts can no more be proved than the existence of the archetypes, so long as they do not manifest themselves concretely.[80]

---

[78] Jung's use of the term "imago" indicates that he refers to the image of the father that takes shape in the child's inner world, not solely derived from one's experience of the personal father.

[79] "The Father in the Destiny of the Individual," *Freud and Psychoanalysis,* CW 4, pars. 728f. (This passage does not appear in the original text from 1909, but was added in the revised edition, 1948. It expresses succinctly the idea of the archetypes, of which nebulous traces can be discerned in the original edition.)

[80] "Psychological Aspects of the Mother Archetype," *The Archetypes and the Collective Unconscious,* CW 9i, par. 155.

As "possibilities of representation," the archetypes manifest only when some level of consciousness comes into play. Thus we find archetypal ideas and images in myths and fairytales, in religion and in literature. Archetypal motifs, for instance the stages of childhood and coming of age, unfold in a person's actual experience. These motifs exist prior to the individual child's development, and whatever unexpected realizations the encounter with old age might bring, there were those who came of age before oneself.

However, what for mankind is a small step might sometimes be a giant leap in one's life. The archetype does not determine one's life course, and the actual experience is not shaped by a predetermined mold. To this end we need complexes, for they are *the path and the vessel that give human shape and structure to archetypal patterns as they unfold in personal experience.* The complexes provide the link between archetype and ego, enabling the transformation of the archetypal into the personal. Just like dreams, which attain their garments from the complexes, writes Jung,

> [Complexes] are not subject to our control but obey their own laws. . . . In saying this, we assume that there are independent psychic complexes which elude our conscious control and come and go according to their own laws.[81]

The complex is, thus, messenger of the gods, or the archetypes, rather than of the ego, though the personal life is its object.

Jacobi calls the complex the "energy-giving cell from which all further psychic life flows,"[82] and "the life-renewing and life-promoting source whose function it is to raise the contents of the unconscious to consciousness and mobilize the formative powers of consciousness."[83]

The complex enables the transition from the land of blueprints and propensities to the personal world of individual experience. Complexes might be imagined as trucks that transport instinctual and archetypal raw material from the never-ending vastness of the great unconscious, bringing it on the long and winding road into the city-boundaries of the "ego-state," in which nature can be further shaped into human and conscious culture. Or, we might imagine the complexes as bubbles that rise up from the ar-

---

[81] "The Psychological Foundations of Belief in Spirits," *The Structure and Dynamics of the Psyche,* CW 8, par. 580.
[82] *Complex/Archetype/Symbol,* p. 27.
[83] Ibid., p. 29.

chetypal world at the bottom of the sea. A complex that can be integrated into the individual's evolving consciousness enables the ego to expand, and the ego boundaries become more flexible. This is the teleological, purposeful task of the complex.

The Complex as Path and Vessel of Transformation

In the Grimm fairy tale "The Three Feathers,"[84] which Marie-Louise von Franz has analyzed so eloquently in *The Interpretation of Fairy Tales,* the old and weak king is thinking of his end.

In order to find out who shall inherit the kingdom, the king sends his three sons, of whom "two were clever and wise, but the third did not speak much, and was simple, and was called the Simpleton," to bring him the most beautiful carpet. He blew three feathers in the air, and said, "You shall go as they fly." Simpleton had to follow the third feather that had not really taken off, but fallen to the ground not far away. Sitting down sad-dened, he suddenly saw a trap door that he opened, with steps leading down to a fat toad. Upon Simpleton's request the toad brings a box from which she gives him a carpet "so beautiful and so fine, that on the earth above, none could have been woven like it."

Simpleton, representing the inferior and neglected principle, has brought his father, the dying king—the dominant but outworn principle of consciousness—the most beautiful carpet. His older but inflated brothers are of course outraged, and demand a new agreement. The father accepts and asks his sons to find the most beautiful ring. He again prompts them to follow the flight of intuition on the wings of the feathers, and Simpleton's lands near the door to the underground. He goes down to the toad, who from her big box gives him a ring "which sparkled with jewels, and was so beautiful no goldsmith on earth would have been able to make it." It was certainly more beautiful than the nails his lazily clever brothers had knocked out of an old carriage-ring. They of course do not accept their defeat, nor do they waste time on introspection, suppressing their Simple-ton complex back into the dust and dirt of their unconscious, not realizing what treasures can be found under the ground.

Next they must bring home the most beautiful woman. Simpleton again descends into the underground and asks the fat toad, the Earth Mother, for help. "Oh," answers the toad, "the most beautiful woman! She is not at

---

[84] *The Complete Grimm's Fairy Tales,* pp. 319ff.

hand at the moment, but still you shall have her." She gives him a yellow turnip (seemingly the swede turnip, *Brassica napus,* with its yellow-fleshed root; von Franz, however, speaks about a carrot), which had been hollowed out, and to which six mice were harnessed. Simpleton asks what to do with it, to which the toad answers, "Just put one of my little toads into it." Then he seizes one at random and puts her into the yellow coach. Hardly is she seated than she turns into a beautiful maiden, and the turnip into a coach, and the six mice into horses.

While victorious again, his brothers of course impose yet another task. Simpleton's maiden and the peasant women the brothers had brought home (which might indicate they are coming closer to the ground, beginning their own process) have to jump through a ring in the center of the hall. The toad turned maiden is of course by far the most gracious one, so Simpleton finally receives the crown and comes to rule wisely "for a length of time."

As long as the new king is vigorous we might expect him to rule wisely. He then truly represents the Self's unfolding in consciousness, still connected to the vitality of the unconscious and the energy of the symbols he has brought up from the underworld. As long as he is in power, the king is the dominant principle of consciousness. He sets the rules of collective consciousness, the generally accepted norms and laws. With time, though, if not constantly scrutinized and rejuvenated, collective consciousness has a tendency to become stale and hardened. The spirit fades, the king is dying, the individual's or society's guiding myth has become obsolete. When not renewed, the dominant of consciousness runs the risk of becoming a lifeless neurotic ego-defense. It becomes phobic or compulsive, like the rites of the soul and rituals of the spirit that have fallen into the ruins of obsessive litany and compulsive decree. Remarkably, it is the complex and the wound that bring renewal, while perfection serves the interest of a rigid and impermeable ego.

Simpleton doesn't speak much; that is, the inferior function is repressed or denied, not recognized by the dominant function of consciousness. The inferior function often serves as a complex at the entrance to our underground shadow. For a stiff and rigid king, for a defensive ego, Simpleton represents a split-off, autonomous complex. While undoubtedly the hero who brings renewal, he is quite unlike any typical hero-ideal. He is also not the hero who ventures far away, who searches for adventure. He is, rather, a "complex-hero." He is close to home, where in fact most of our complexes reside. Whether locked in the basement or projected onto our neighbors, we want to know nothing of them.

Von Franz amplifies the meaning of the feathers as wind, hint, imagination, letting one's thoughts wander. That is, the feathers show us where psychic energy is heading. In order to approach the unconscious and bring renewal therefrom, we need to loosen up, which the flight of the feather in the wind enables. To be stuck in routine and the conventions of collective consciousness, as the lazy ego often is, means to be arrogant to the wind,[85] to the new, to the different, and certainly to our complexes. They then take us by surprise. When turning on us unexpectedly, complexes of course become more wounding than when adequately accounted for.

The archetypes are blueprints, but they do not have fingerprints. Empty and purely formal, archetypes lack the complexity of individual life. But also an ego stiffened by identification with the persona and with collective consciousness, concerned with correct behavior and how things "should" be, disconnects from its roots in the unconscious and comes to lack complexity. The carpet that the king asked for, says von Franz, "is often used as a symbol for the complex symbolic patterns of life and the secret designs of fate."[86] She adds that "this purposiveness of an individual life-pattern, which gives one a feeling of meaningfulness, is very often symbolized in the carpet." For the Jew, during centuries of migration, the unrolling of the carpet in a new place represented a personalized fragment of territory, a tangible connection to the archetypal, ancestral ground.

Von Franz speaks of the ring that the sons are asked to bring as expressing "an eternal connection through the Self."[87] Only by recognizing our connection with the Self and the archetypes of the unconscious are we fully living. It is the instrumental task of the complex to provide this link. This of course entails the inevitable paradox, that only through imperfection, and recognition of it (by encountering our shadow), can we constructively relate to the divine spark within. "The perfect have no need of others," notes Jung.[88] The perfect need no other person, nor do they assume

---

[85] *Wind* and *soul/spirit* are one word in Hebrew, *ruah.* Bob Dylan, "blowin' in the wind," knew well where to search for the answer.

[86] *The Interpretation of Fairy Tales,* p. 56.

[87] Ibid., p. 59.

[88] "The Undiscovered Self," *Civilization in Transition,* CW 10, par. 579.

they need an inner other—neither shadow nor Self. Confident that they can manage without the other, they often come to wound the other, whether inner or outer.

In "The Three Feathers," as in so many other tales, the maiden, the anima, is absent, asleep or deceased. In fact, it is quite natural that the anima, the soul, has to be constantly redeemed. When natural relatedness, after having become conscious morality, turns into kingly commands and regulations to be meticulously and uncritically obeyed, then the anima has been sacrificed, relinquished rather than sanctified. This tale does not tell about an anima that serves as a guide into the realm of the unconscious. Here, rather, she is the soul that can bring life and vitality into consciousness, on condition that she is looked for, and looked after, which the elder brothers do not do. The absence of the purposeful complex may lie at the core of many childhood conflicts. Freud states it thus, when summing up the case of the Wolf Man,

> The contradictions between experience and the [phylogenetically inherited] schema seem to supply the conflicts of childhood with an abundance of material.[89]

The inferior function of the ego, Simpleton, cooperates with the creative aspect of the unconscious, the life-giving Earth Mother. The essence of the complex is the mice- and horse-driven coach. The complex is the structure, the carriage, wherein archetypal and instinctual patterns take shape and can make the journey to the surface to manifest in the human sphere. From empty and purely formal possibilities in the collective unconscious, the archetypes can begin to take animal shape, for instance as a toad, in the womb of the Earth Mother. Here they are close enough to the human sphere to be comprehended, and to exert a pull on the ego. The inferior function, by means of which our ego reaches down into the shadow, can be activated. The new material to be brought to the surface, into the kingdom of conscious identity, has to be searched for, because "she is not at hand." When pulled from the round, that is, when a partly conscious choice is brought to bear on the primordial shape of the circle, psychic movement can begin.[90]

This is what we do when we attend to dreams. In partial consciousness

---

[89] "From the History of an Infantile Neurosis," SE 17, pp. 119f.
[90] See Erich Neumann, *The Origins and History of Consciousness*, pp.275ff.

we may take down a dream that has been written in our unconscious. In the carriage, the vehicle that brings unconscious contents to the surface, into consciousness, the toad is transformed into a maiden. In von Franz's version the vehicle is a carrot, and she emphasizes its phallic character. A turnip, round in shape, would be more feminine. Von Franz says that "the vehicle bringing up the anima is sex and sexual fantasy."[91] Clearly, whether male or female, the complex carries sexual energy, which is its life-enhancing engine.[92]

The energic element of the complex, as transformative vessel of instinctual and archetypal material, is particularly evident in its being driven by mice- and horse-power—instinctual shadow energy. Mice generally refer to the powers of darkness, "gnawing at the root of the Tree of Life."[93] They evoke anxiety and "nocturnal worries."[94] Or, in Kafka's words,

> My reaction towards the mice is one of sheer terror. To analyze its source would be the task of the psychoanalyst, which I am not. Certainly, this fear, like an insect phobia, is connected with the unsuspected, uninvited, inescapable, more or less silent, persistent, secret aims of these creatures, with the sense that they have riddled the surrounding walls through and through with their tunnels and are lurking within, that the night is theirs, that because of their nocturnal existence and their tininess they are so remote from us and thus outside our power.[95]

Kafka's nightly mice disturb quiet sleep, evoking night's other son, death—which might be seen as life's "silent, persistent" and inescapable "secret aim." As Freud notes,

> If we are to take it as a truth that knows no exception that everything living dies for *internal* reasons—becomes inorganic once again—then we shall be compelled to say that *"the aim of all life is death."*[96]

The complex's engine is initially driven by the power of death-anxiety, the sheer terror of the unintended and inescapable. This annihilatory anxi-

---

[91] *The Interpretation of Fairy Tales*, p. 63.

[92] See the discussion on Oedipus as "Swollen Foot," below, pp. 44f., 57f.

[93] J.C. Cooper, *An Illustrated Encyclopaedia of Traditional Symbols*, p. 110.

[94] *The Interpretation of Fairy Tales*, p. 64.

[95] Franz Kafka, *Letters To Friends, Family, and Editors*, p. 174.

[96] *Beyond the Pleasure Principle*, SE 18, p. 38.

ety that like mice gnaws into the matter of life, is then deflected into "horsepower," the hero's vital animal energy,[97] by means of which he can fight the dragon that carries the death-anxiety. This is the more forceful, aggressive, martial energy. Thus, Eros, Mars and Thanatos come together to "drive" the complex, to actuate the archetypal possibilities of representation into human shape and complexity. Complexes are the carriers of life energy, enabling archetypal energy to bear on the personal. Archetypal energy is thereby transformed into living reality, instead of remaining buried in the unconscious embrace of the Great Mother, or burning as forbidden flame in the sphere of the Spiritual Father. When the ego rejects and refuses to integrate the complex, the complex becomes autonomous, split-off, and will detract energy from the ego, rather than promote the transformation of archetype into ego. Until finding its identity, the swan remains an ugly duckling, but having gone through the winter of rejection, the spring of ego-acceptance brings new life:

> Even the elder tree bent its branches straight down into the water before him, and the sun shone warm and mild. Then his wings rustled, he lifted his slender neck, and cried rejoicingly from the depths of his heart, "I never dreamed of so much happiness when I was still the ugly Duckling!"[98]

An adequately ego-integrated complex brings new energy. For the sake of clarity, however, it should be emphasized that the ego should not usurp everything archetypal. The ego's desire to do so amounts to the pathology of hubris. Particularly, complexes with an archetypal overload, notes Jung, will cause severe pathology if they enter the sphere of the ego.

> While the contents of the personal unconscious are felt as belonging to one's own psyche, the contents of the collective unconscious seem alien, as if they came from outside. The re-integration of a personal complex has the effect of release and often of healing, whereas the invasion of a complex from the collective unconscious is a very disagreeable and even dangerous phenomenon. The parallel with the primitive belief in souls and spirits is obvious: souls correspond to the autonomous complexes of the personal unconscious, and spirits to those of the collective unconscious.[99]

---

[97] See *Symbols of Transformation,* CW 5, par. 616.

[98] Hans Christian Andersen, "The Ugly Duckling," in *The Complete Illustrated Works,* p. 163.

[99] "The Psychological Foundations of Belief in Spirits," *The Structure and Dynamics of the Psyche,* CW 8, par. 591.

Core, Cluster and Tone

Jung describes a feeling-toned complex as

> the *image* of a certain psychic situation which is strongly accentuated emotionally. . . . This image has a powerful inner coherence, it has its own wholeness and, in addition, a relatively high degree of autonomy, so that it is subject to the control of the conscious mind to only a limited extent.[100]

Complex denotes a network of *associations*, images, ideas, memories, or the like, clustered around a nuclear, *archetypal core* of meaning, and characterized and held together by a common *emotional tone*.[101]

Thus, the complex embodies three major elements—an archetypal core around which personal experiences cluster, and an emotional tone that serves as the gravitational force that holds this microcosm together.

The nuclear core is archetypal

At the center of every complex stands an archetype. Any archetype—such as father, mother, child; *puer-senex* (youth-old age); hubris, the archetype of inflation; nemesis, the archetype of proportions; the birth-death-rebirth theme of transformation, and so on—can form the nuclear core of a complex. The myth of Oedipus is a narrative of an archetypal theme that constitutes the core of a complex that, according to Freud, is reexperienced universally in stages of development.

The archetypal image at its core conveys the essence of meaning of the complex. The image of the sick old man may represent the frailty of the anima, in her capacity as "the breath of life," without which the body is an empty wrapping around a hardened heart. In the sick old man, the life-principle is ailing, as expressed for instance in the symptoms of disease that compound in complexes of hypochondria.

For example, some months after the start of analysis, a forty-year-old man, suffering from somatic symptoms and physical neglect, starts to dream repeatedly of his sister. Initially he beats her violently, usually in the street. Eventually he brings her home. Once she takes a bath, another time he invites her to eat. This dreamer has no sister, nor a female (or male) partner, so the dream images cannot be interpreted on the objective

---

[100] "A Review of the Complex Theory," *The Structure and Dynamics of the Psyche*, CW 8, par. 201.

[101] See A. Samuels, B. Shorter and F. Plaut, eds., *A Critical Dictionary of Jungian Analysis*, p. 34.

level, but must be taken subjectively, as internal objects. The crystallization of the sister-image reflects a beginning relationship to his anima. In fact, before the archetypal core of the anima emerged on the stage of this man's psyche, she resided solely in his preconscious soma, where she was unrelated to or rendered meaningless. Only as she surfaced from his bodily unconscious, taking the shape of complexes in his dream life, could the contours of the anima as archetypal image be detected and its meaning of relatedness unfold. That is, the archetypal core of the anima did exist, though she had not yet come alive. His anima complex had not moved beyond its primary existence in the body. It remained autonomous, split-off, until aggressive energy started to shake life into it through hostile dreams (needless to say, symbolic images are essential to the psyche, and become unforgivably acted out when denied). Eros, relatedness, then followed, as the complex brought life to the archetypal core of the anima.

The cluster is personal

The associations, ideas, memories, etc., that cluster around the archetypal core emanate from a person's encounter with his or her environment and actual childhood experiences, that is, with the personal mother, father, etc. This encounter, obviously, may be of a benevolent or a malevolent nature. The environment will be "good enough" if it can hold the constellated archetype and enable it to unfold into living, personal reality.

Sometimes, however, the environment fails to do so. Imagine being under the spell of love, the archetype of love having taken possession of you in all its numinosity, and the Other as an actual, living person is absent. Disconnection from the archetype (of love, for example) leads to feelings of emptiness and death. Likewise, the presence of the archetype (again, of love, for instance) but the absence of the possibility to carry it into living reality, inevitably leads to feelings of loneliness and estrangement. Another example is the archetype of mother, which embodies the substance of materialization. The archetype of mother and child may have constellated, but a child is not born or cannot be adopted. In such a case the archetype does not unfold in living reality. Or, conversely, the birth of a child does not necessarily mean that the archetype becomes constellated in the sphere of the personal. The person everyone now calls mother may be unable to attach to the feeling and the sensation. The archetype of mother has not unfolded in that person. The lack of a sense of mother sometimes compounds in the agony of post-partum depression.

There is a need for the constellation of a human, personal, holding environment to provide the child with a cluster of experiences, interactions and impressions. Within this good-enough, holding environment, archetypal themes can unfold and become personalized. For instance, the archetypes of annihilatory chaos as well as paradisiacal harmony may be lived out in the human sphere, in proportions and in such a way that they can be held and coped with. The fear of the devouring night may be held at bay within the confines of secure and good-enough parenting. Telling a story, holding the hand, stroking the head, will soften the exposure to the frightening dark. Thus, a human presence mitigates the otherwise awesome impact of the archetypes, in whose vicinity the small child lives. The complex constitutes the path of transformation from archetype to human reality, and when exposure is too harsh, the mediating path of complexes may be overrun. Direct, unmediated exposure to the archetypal world becomes traumatic and pathogenic, as in cases of early loss or abuse.

In the youthful puer, who becomes father almost by accident, we often notice the absence of father. In the puer aeternus (eternal youth) the father archetype is not constellated. It is pushed aside by the puer archetype that possesses him. When his wife is due to give birth he is off with his mistress, or forgets to take his wife to hospital, coming home late from meeting his friends at the pub. As we know, this may drive the child to a perpetual search for the absent father, sometimes compulsively projecting into every adult man the caring father that he or she as a child tried to discover behind the actual father. How often do we not hear of a weak, sociopathic, violent father being idealized. This may be the expression of a child's father complex that labors hard to find the positive archetypal elements of father, such as guidance and sincerity, behind the denial and repression of the unsatisfactory experience of the personal father.

Or, one may develop a negative father complex, where the idea (archetype) of father takes on an entirely negative color and tone. In such a case, all adult men who may be conceived of as carrying the archetype of father—managers, judges, men in authority positions—are seen as bad, illwilled, violent, deceitful, and preferably avoided. Yet, as is characteristic of the complex, they are encountered repeatedly and compulsively.

So while on one end of the complex we find its essential and meaningful archetypal core, at the other end the complex gains its character from actual life experiences.

The feeling-tone

The feeling-tone of the complex, that is, its characteristic emotional tone, is the glue that holds it together. Already early on, Jung became aware of the centrality of the emotional charge or feeling-tone of the complex. Describing a research subject, he writes:

> Attention is completely bound up with the inner, emotionally charged complex, from which she cannot detach herself. . . . Her attention is thus abnormally low for anything that does not concern the complex. [102]

Symptomatically, the emotional charge becomes unmistakably apparent through affect. An autonomous complex is like an infected wound, and when touched, triggered, activated, *constellated*, we are affected, as evidenced by an exaggerated emotional response; for instance, oversensitivity, feelings of sadness, outbursts of anger or embarrassment, etc.

The feeling-tone of the complex not only holds the network of experiences together around the nuclear core, it also ensures that the complex is dynamic and energetic. It is the life force of the complex—we might say, the anima of the complex.

The feeling-tone must also be considered in the context of Jung's model of typology and his definition of the feeling function, which has to do with relationship and value. As Jung says,

> Feeling is primarily a process . . . that imparts to the content a definite *value* in the sense of acceptance or rejection ("like" or "dislike"). The process can also appear isolated, as it were, in the form of a "mood . . . .
>
> Feeling, therefore, is an entirely *subjective* process . . . . When the intensity of feeling increases, it turns into an *affect,* i.e., a feeling-state accompanied by marked physical innervations. Feeling is distinguished from affect by the fact that it produces no perceptible physical innervations, i.e., neither more nor less than an ordinary thinking process.[103]

Feeling is the matter, the substance and the concern, of relatedness. It pertains to the way people relate to each other, but also to how the archetypal core relates to an external event, and what value one ascribes to the event, the act, the behavior, or the person involved.

For example, a man, let's call him Samuel, might on the spur of the moment decide to visit a close friend, only to find he is not at home. He

---

[102] "Studies in Word Association," *Experimental Researches,* CW 2, par. 167.
[103] "Definitions," *Psychological Types,* CW 6, pars. 724f.

might appropriately think, "What a pity, I took a chance. I would like to have seen him, but I shall call him later." However, since Samuel suffers from an abandonment complex, the archetypal core image of the abandoned child is constellated. The external event is assimilated into a cluster of associations, and his friend's absence joins an endless string of real and imaginary situations in which Samuel has found himself feeling abandoned, lonely, homeless, knocking on people's doors, not being let in. The image of the orphan within him is constellated. He feels lonely in the dark and rainy evening, while everybody else hides together behind the lights of their warm homes. This is the theme of, among others, Hans Christian Andersen's poignant tale of "The Little Match Girl," who barefoot and bereft walks the cold winter streets on New Year's Eve, seeing food and warm lights in every house (see below, page 86).

Especially when complexes are unconscious, their power of assimilation is accentuated. The autonomous complex may, similar to the conscious ego, assimilate experiences and integrate them into its bulk of memories and associations, In the extreme, a complex may assimilate the ego. This is known as identification with the complex, which, as Jung says, in "the Middle Ages . . . was called possession."[104]

The feeling that an external situation triggers, that is, how it is related to and the value ascribed to it, determines whether a complex is constellated or not. Jung emphasizes that *"the constellating power of the nuclear element corresponds to its value intensity, i.e., to its energy."*[105]

When constellated, activated, the complex will assimilate the new event into its sphere, into its cluster of memories and associations.

Jung introduced the concept of *imago* in order to differentiate the subjective image of a person or situation from its objective reality:

> The psychic image of an object is never exactly like the object—at most there is a near resemblance. . . . In practical psychology, therefore, we would do well to make a rigorous distinction between the image or *imago* of a man and his real existence. Because of its extremely subjective origin, the *imago* is frequently more an image of a subjective functional complex than of the object itself.[106]

---

[104] "A Review of the Complex Theory," *The Structure and Dynamics of the Psyche,* CW 8, par. 204.
[105] "On Psychic Energy," ibid., par. 19.
[106] "Definitions," *Psychological Types,* CW 6, par. 812.

That is, the object is not simply internalized. Father or mother are not external objects that are incorporated wholesale into the complex. The object is related to and evaluated according to intrapsychic factors that will color them and change their shape, consistency and structure. Thus, a strict and demanding father may be perceived by one of his sons as a trustworthy mentor who guides him in the puzzling ways of society, while the other son may revolt against what he feels to be excessive control. This is the conflict, as found in many myths, between the first-born son and the second-born. We all have a first-born as well as a second-born within us, where the latter at some stage has to overcome the first-born, so that the person may acquire an independent position in life, separate from the internalized image of the father.

Thus, the child's father-*imago*, its inner idea of father, is not only an internalization of the actual father, and of the father's complexes, and of the mother's animus and her father complex, but a fusion between the internalized object and the externalized archetype.

Archetype and Ego

Under healthy circumstances, there is an ongoing dialogue between the personal and the archetypal, between the individual and the universal. It is the task of the complex to link them, to ensure this dialogue. In psychosis the archetypal world has taken possession of the ego, and in neurosis the ego has disconnected from its archetypal roots. Psychic health may be discerned when the two dimensions are balanced as well as differentiated.

The craftsman is a pertinent image, often found in myth and religion, of the tedious and patient labor that enables the Self's unfolding in consciousness, which is the purposeful work of the complex. He replicates the divine on earth, by skill, patience, carefulness and hard work, willing to let the archetypal be carved out in the physical reality of his workshop.

The human body is an archetypal blueprint, with a universal outline of head, torso, arms, legs and genitals, front and back. The archetype in itself, however, cannot be seen. It remains a possibility that needs to be represented. No one ever saw a body in its stylistic, archetypal outline without being fleshed out by the personal, complex dimension.

Inborn as well as acquired features, such as one's actual face and fingerprints, but also the bending of one's back due to the burdens of one's life, the fear or the joy in one's eyes, wrinkles and strains, heaviness or swiftness of movement, pertain to the complexity of individual life rather than the universality of the archetypes.

There is to everything both an archetypal and a complex dimension. All structures of the psyche have an archetypal as well as complex bearing. The complex brings variation to the typicality of the archetype. If, for example, we assume a universality of ego as center of consciousness in the psyche, then the ego is the central archetype of consciousness, just as the Self is the central archetype of the entire psyche.

As the ego manifests in human reality, we often speak of the ego complex. Experiences and images gather, or cluster, around the nuclear, archetypal idea of consciousness. In terms of Jung's model of typology, by means of the four functions of consciousness—*thinking* (defining) and *feeling* (relation and value), *sensation* (distinguishing the facts) and *intuition* (detecting the possibilities)—experiences and images are drawn into and constellate personal consciousness, the ego complex.

Even though dream images may be viewed along a spectrum from archetypal, where we rarely obtain particular associations but rather sense their numinosity, to personal, both dimensions are always present. Just as the archetypes are the inhabitants of the collective unconscious, the complexes inhabit our personal unconscious.[107] By means of the complexes the archetypal images receive personal dress.

When a man dreams of walking down "Samson Street," say, to meet his sick and ailing father, we naturally attend to his personal associations, which lead to his complexes. But we do well to try to grasp the archetypal significance as well. Thus, Samson Street on a personal level may be the main thoroughfare in his childhood neighborhood. But Samson (whose name means "strength of the sun") is an archetypal image of a sun-hero. Ergo, the dreamer must walk down the heroic road of childhood retrospection. He must come to terms with his sick father, but he must also meet the old and ailing father or king within himself.

In fact this is a true example. Like Samson, the male principle weighed heavily on this analysand, who through regular weight-lifting had developed impressive muscles, leaving little space for genuine relations. Easily seduced and easily betrayed, he recurrently found himself impotent and lonely, abandoned by one Delilah after another. By dressing archetypal

---

[107] See "The Concept of the Collective Unconscious," *The Archetypes and the Collective Unconscious*, CW 9i, pars. 88ff.

images in the clothes of personified complexes, the dream seemed to prompt this man to address his problems.

From bipolarity to good enough

While the archetypes are fundamentally bipolar, they often split as we conceive of them as images, for instance in fairy tales. The mother archetype, for instance, entails aspects of devouring and death as well as love and nurturing. In her virtuous aspects we find her as the good fairy, while we might see the terrible side of the archetype in the wicked stepmother, witch or hag. The polarities of father are noticeable in images such as the cruel king and the poor but caring farmer.

D.W. Winnicott is the brilliant interpreter of Jung's ideas on the level of personal psychology.[108] As human beings we are less stereotypical than archetypal images—not all good, not all bad, but hopefully good enough. The personal always carries the burden of imperfection, that is, of our complexes. The good-enough mother, who nurtures and frustrates, pertains to the sphere of real, actual life. She is by nature more complex than the archetypal mother, the Great Mother, the goddess. "Good enough" means being human, not greater than life, and represents the human attempt to hold the archetypal poles without identification with the one while repressing the other into the shadow. A good-enough human being is someone far less than perfect, able to carry his or her wounds and complexes, neither possessed by archetypal identification nor in the grips of autonomous complexes, which by nature thrive on splitting—either good or bad, never simply good enough.

Dismemberment

Like any idea that takes shape in the actual world, archetypes when unfolding in the personal psyche reveal themselves in less pure form. They become more complex. If Aphrodite is an archetypal image of love, then we are blessed and possessed by her when falling in love. In love we feel the spell and the numinosity of the archetype. As we grow up, we tend to climb up and out of the love we have fallen into. In doing this, we *dismember* Aphrodite. This is similar to Erich Neumann's notion of frag-

---

[108] See, for instance, *Playing And Reality*. For example, "It fell to my lot to be a psychoanalyst who . . . sensed the importance of this universal [phenomenon] in the lives of infants and children." pp. xif.

mentation of the archetype and "secondary personalization,"[109] and Michael Fordham's concept of "deintegration."[110]

Dismemberment—cutting into pieces, differentiating and discarding— is the complex process by which we separate from the archetypes, establish a differentiated ego, and discard the unacceptable into the shadow of the personal unconscious (which takes shape together with the ego).

Later on, a fragmented ego, disconnected from its roots in the Self, may need re-memberment, that is, integration of its different members, organs, complexes. The myth of Isis and Osiris describes the cycle of dismemberment/re-memberment, and in the fairy tale "Fitcher's Bird"[111] (or, as it is sometimes called, "Fowler's Fowl"[112]), the cycle is strongly associated with childhood.

In therapy this process usually begins by re-membering childhood, not only because childhood is the place of complex-formation and the splitting-off of autonomous complexes, but also because the child is closer to the Self. If we completely abandon archetypal Aphrodite, she becomes embittered, leaving us loveless, fragmented, indifferent to and inconsiderate of the other—inner as well as outer. We lose touch with the archetypal energies and dry up. In the tale of Amor and Psyche, when men abandon the cult of Aphrodite they turn to the maiden Psyche, the nascent human soul, not boundaryless like Aphrodite, but confined within its own limitations.[113] When the archetype unfolds in empirical, personal life, it loses its totality as well as some or much of its numinosity. The grandness and wholeness of Heavenly Jerusalem shatters on earthly ground; the dream and fantasy of Eternal Peace as a replica of postnatal union with the protective and nurturing Great Mother shatters in the reality of warring opposites of human existence. This is, as well, the loss of omnipotence and omnipotent projections.

While the carriers of archetypal projections, whether parents or lovers, initially may be endowed with archetypal mana, extraordinary charisma, there inevitably follows a process of deintegration by which we become humanized, differentiated and replete with wounds and shortcomings. This

[109] *The Origins and History of Consciousness*, pp. 335ff.

[110] See, for instance, Samuels, *Jung And the Post-Jungians*, pp. 154ff.

[111] *The Complete Grimm's Fairy Tales*, pp. 216ff.

[112] *Grimm's Grimmest*, pp. 84ff.

[113] See Erich Neumann, *Amor and Psyche*, pp. 3f., 58f.

is the task of the complex, as the personal traits and features are carved out of the archetypal sculpture along the path of individual experiences and relations. It is often quite painful as projected images collapse in living relationships, but it enables partners to be human and imperfect.

The godlike child that has to carry his or her parents' archetypal hopes and fears is unable to mature as an individual, but instead remains puerile or is caught up in narcissistic emptiness.

When we speak about complexes we usually think of problems and pathology. This pertains to the autonomous complex, which forms one nodal point of looking at psychopathology from a Jungian perspective (another one being the ego-Self axis). The autonomous complex comes into being when the purposeful task of complexes fails, for instance due to the ego's inability to assimilate or integrate the complex. Then it becomes autonomous, a development further explored here in chapter four.

3
Oedipus and the Archetypal Complex

Freud, Jung and Oedipus

The Oedipus myth constitutes the guiding myth of Freudian thinking, which is focused on psychosexual development and genital maturity. By letting Oedipus carry the burden of illustrating the process and the structure of the complexes according to Jungian theory, I inevitably associate myself with those who, said Freud, deprive "the complex of its value through twisted re-interpretations."[114]

It was not until 1910 that Freud gave the name Oedipus to his nuclear core complex, although by then he had been preoccupied with it for years. He first mentions the idea in a letter to Wilhelm Fliess, October 15, 1897, written during the self-analysis he undertook after his father's death:

> One single thought of general value has been revealed to me. I have found, in my own case too, [the phenomenon of] falling in love with the mother and jealousy of the father, and I now regard it as a universal event of early childhood . . . .
>
> We can understand the riveting power of Oedipus Rex . . . the Greek legend seizes on a compulsion which everyone recognizes because he feels its existence within himself.[115]

Much later, in 1949, Freud further emphasized Oedipus' significance:

> If psychoanalysis could boast of no other achievement than the discovery of the repressed Oedipus complex, that alone would give it a claim to be included among the precious new acquisitions of mankind.[116]

The resolution of the Oedipus complex is the primary aim of Freudian analysis. Maturity is achieved by the release of libido from its fixations, whereby freed-up energy can be put at the disposal of the ego, enabling it to love and work. To quote Freud, "Every new arrival on this planet is faced with the task of mastering the Oedipus complex."[117] Failure to do so

---

[114] *Introductory Lectures on Psychoanalysis,* SE 15, pp. 207f.

[115] "Extracts from the Fliess Papers," SE 1, p. 265.

[116] *An Outline of Psychoanalysis,* SE 23, pp. 192f.

[117] *Three Essays on the Theory of Sexuality,* SE 7, p. 226, note 1.

results in neurosis, and is "one of the most important sources of the sense of guilt by which neurotics are so often tormented."[118]

In Jungian psychology, abundant with complexes, it is, however, a neglected complex. Jung was resistant to it, perhaps because of his own "wishing-the-father-dead" complex, which clearly has more than an Oedipal slant to it. When asked about the Oedipus complex, he said,

> That is just what I call an archetype. It was the first archetype Freud discovered, the first and only one. He thought this *was* the archetype. Of course there are many such archetypes.[119]

While there are indeed many archetypes, Oedipus stands out as the archetypal configuration of complexes.

Complexes are essential to the development of the individual personality. Consequently, Jung places the Oedipus complex firmly in childhood. In a brief lecture on the subject, he says,

> Thanks to the concerted efforts of the psychoanalytic school, we have discovered that the most frequent fantasy of childhood is the so-called Oedipus complex.[120]

However, Jung promptly de-emphasizes the sexual aspect:

> This weakening and reduction in scale of the Oedipus complex should not be understood as a diminution of the total sum of affect, but as indicating the smaller share of sexual affect characteristic of a child. . . .
> . . . . Of course, for the child itself, the mother at this early stage of childhood has no sexual significance worth mentioning, and to that extent the term "Oedipus complex" is not really suitable.[121]

This lecture dates from 1912—that is, at a time when his relationship with Freud was coming to an end. Jung ends it by stating,

> [Freud] calls this complex the root-complex, or nucleus, of the neuroses and is inclined, viewing this as the original one, to reduce practically the whole psychology of the neuroses, as well as many other phenomena in the realm of the mind, to this one complex.[122]

---

[118] *Introductory Lectures on Psychoanalysis*, SE 16, p. 332.
[119] "The Houston Films," in McGuire and Hull, *C.G. Jung Speaking*, pp. 288f.
[120] "The Theory of Psychoanalysis," *Freud and Psychoanalysis*, CW 4, par. 343.
[121] Ibid., pars. 344f.
[122] Ibid., par. 352.

Only in the following lecture, however, does he strike a definite chord against Oedipus, slaying him, so to speak, at least in his capacity as messenger of neurosis:

> The point is that the *regression of libido abolishes to a very large extent the aetiological significance of childhood experiences.* It had seemed to us very peculiar anyway that the Oedipus or Electra complex should have a determining influence in the formation of a neurosis, since these complexes are actually present in everyone.[123]

Following Jung's assertion that the complex is "present in everyone" but is not a determinant of neurosis, we might view Oedipus not as the harbinger of the autonomous complex—though he seems to be driven by one—but rather as the carrier of the purposeful task of the complex. While he, partly and certainly neurotically, fulfils the task of driving the archetype into the realm of the ego, he fails to create a self-related ego. This is, however, not the task of the complex.

The Myth of Oedipus

Laius, king of Thebes, had been warned three times by the oracle that were he to have a son by Jocasta, that son would kill him. The oracle had cautioned him:

> Sow no offspring against the will of the gods! You will produce a son who will slay you and annihilate in blood your entire house.

But passion and wine overcame Laius, and a son was born. To release himself from his fate, he pierced the infant's feet and gave him over to shepherds to be exposed, that is, to be abandoned outside the city-walls, left unprotected in a jar, in wintertime. However, the shepherds gave the infant to Periboea, wife of Polybus, king of Corinth. They brought the boy up as their own and named him Oedipus, "Swollen Foot."

As a young man, redheaded Oedipus easily burst into fits of rage. One day, at a banquet in the palace, he was taunted by a drunken guest for not being a true son of mild King Polybus. This accusation troubled him, and he went to Delphi to inquire of the oracle if it were true. The Pythia, without waiting to hear his question, drove him ardently away from Apollo's shrine, crying out that he would kill his father and marry his mother. In horror Oedipus turned eastward, intending never to return to his parents in

---

[123] Ibid., par. 377.

Corinth. He became a lonely and homeless wanderer.

On his way, Oedipus came to a crossroad, "The Cleft Way," or "The Triple Way" as it was also called. At such godforsaken crossroads where three ways converge, Hecate, goddess of the dark and moonless night, and her pack of ghostly hounds of hell would haunt the traveler. If not related to appropriately, if not paid due respect, the threshold experience provided by the crossroads of life becomes insignificant, trivial. As Karl Kerényi says, "The crossroads themselves were the fate."[124]

At the Cleft Way crossroad, where the road that descends from Delphi cleaves, one of the routes leads to Thebes. There Oedipus came across a man in a chariot and was commanded, "Traveler, make way for the king!" Oedipus, boiling with rage, refused. He assumed they were a band of robbers and declared that he knew no betters except the gods and his own parents. The charioteer urged his horses forward, and a wheel of the car rolled over Oedipus' already swollen foot. The old king struck Oedipus on the head with the forked goad he used to drive his entourage. Infuriated, Oedipus took his staff and struck dead the rider and the king, bit into the body of the dead man and spat out his blood.

Oedipus reached Thebes and found the city in turmoil. The Sphinx, that dreadful monster with a woman's head and breasts, the body of a lion and the wings of a bird, had settled herself on the walls of the citadel, the city's protecting fortress. She killed the Thebans one by one, strangling them to death.[125] The last victim had been Haemon, son of Creon, who acted as regent for Laius, who had left for Delphi, to inquire of the oracle how to save the city.

Before killing her victims the Sphinx asked them a riddle:

> There is a two-footed creature on the earth, and a four-footed one called by the same name, and also a three-footed one. It alone of all living creatures that dwell on the earth, in the air, and in the sea changes its form.

---

[124] "Oedipus: Two Essays," in Carl Kerényi and James Hillman, *Oedipus Variations: Studies in Literature and Psychoanalysis*, p. 11.

[125] *Sphinx* means "throttler." To throttle (cf. throat) means to choke or strangle. Thus, the Sphinx may be related to Ananke, goddess of necessity, "she who determines life from the beginning" (James Hillman, "On the Necessity of Abnormal Psychology," in *Facing the Gods*, p. 16)—that is, Fate. Ananke is etymologically related to angina and anxiety, and to *chenek* in Hebrew and other Semitic languages, likewise meaning to choke or to strangle.

The Thebans would be free from this plague when someone would answer the riddle rightly. Creon offered the hand of his sister Jocasta, widow of Laius, and a share in the kingdom to any man who could save the city from the Sphinx. Oedipus gave this answer to the Sphinx's riddle:

> Man is what you mean, since after he is born he crawls around on the earth and is four-footed, walks upright in his prime, but when he becomes old, he bears a crooked neck under the load of old age and leans on his staff for the third foot.

The monstrous Sphinx flung herself to death from the walls of the citadel, into the sea. Oedipus was greeted as a hero and made king of Thebes. Shortly after this a lone survivor of Laius' retinue returned. Alarmed at finding Oedipus reigning, he announced that unknown highwaymen had killed the king, and asked to become a shepherd far away from the city.

When Oedipus had reigned for nearly two decades, a terrible plague descended on Thebes. People were dying throughout the country, and the flocks and birds and fruits of the field were destroyed as well. King Oedipus sent Creon to Delphi to inquire about the cause. Creon was told the reason for the plague was that the murderer of Laius lived unpunished in the city. The seer Teiresias was consulted, and the survivor of Laius' company, now a shepherd, and the shepherd who had turned Oedipus over to Polybus, testified. When the truth was discovered—that Oedipus had killed his father and married his mother—Jocasta hanged herself and Oedipus jabbed out his eyes with one of her brooches.

Exiled, Oedipus wandered for many years as an outcast, accompanied by his faithful daughter Antigone, as told by Sophocles in *Oedipus at Colonus*.[126]

Hero and Complex

The image of the hero represents the psychological capacity to respond to a call,[127] to go forth from the conventions of the ego and redeem a treasure that lies dormant, hidden in the unconscious. The hero, then, brings the treasure home into his own individual consciousness or the consciousness of the collective, thereby stimulating social and individual renewal.

The hero is the ego's capacity to turn toward and connect with the Self,

---

[126] For a psychological commentary on Oedipus' later life, see Edward F. Edinger, *The Psyche on Stage,*, pp. 83ff.

[127] See Joseph Campbell, *The Hero with a Thousand Faces,* pp. 49ff.

to venture into the darkness of the shadow and bring forth instinctual and archetypal energies from the depths. To obtain the treasures of the unconscious, which hold what is lacking in ego-consciousness, such as a lost sense of soul or spirit, the hero must struggle with witches and sorcerers, with the gods as well as the obstacles that obstruct his way.

Prometheus, for example, is a hero who suffers greatly for his grand act of affronting the gods by stealing the fire, wrestling it out of their hands and bringing it down to human ground. That is, he brings the archetypal into the realm of the personal, the divine to the human. For this he is severely punished, Zeus' eagle picking at his liver every night for thousands of years. Plato tells us that God "placed in the liver the seat of divination."[128] Prometheus has used the gall, the secretion of the "seat of the divine"—that is, of the Self—to deflect the fire from Self to ego, from the divine into human consciousness. This act of defiance against the gods, essential to man's process of separation/individuation, brings with it the "gnawing" sense of guilt, eternal picking at the seat of life.

Prometheus, moreover, means "forethinker." The Promethean fire indicates the capacity to *plan* the use of that natural transformative energy, fire. When still raging in the unconscious, fire is no less likely to be destructive than constructive, bipolar like everything archetypal. By forethinking mankind can contain the fire and use it to its benefit, to create consciousness and acculturation, warmth and relatedness, heating and cooking, creating new materials and new ideas. His name discloses what in Prometheus's character makes him into a hero. Prometheus is an archetypal image of the formation of the ego complex.[129]

What is it in the character of Oedipus that makes him a hero? Two distinct features, both of which are essential to the theory of complexes.

The initial feature is rooted in the two energies with which he is identified: Mars and Eros, aggression and relatedness, murder and incest. The

---

[128] George R. Elder, *The Body,* p. 269.

[129] The truth of the matter is that Prometheus is not alone. Carrying the burden of the world on one's shoulders, as Prometheus's brother Atlas does, and acting before thinking, like his brother Epimetheus, are necessary as well for the formation of ego and consciousness. The unrestrained curiosity of his sister-in-law, Pandora, also promotes consciousness and scientific progress, too often on account of more careful forethinking. But most evil by far is when man's inflated ego is fired by belief in perfect superiority and in burning hatred destroys his split-off, projected shadow. All is then set on fire, which is the etymological meaning of "holocaust."

other feature is to be found in the nature of his name, later to reappear in his answer to the riddle. We shall later return to his name and to the riddle of the Sphinx, but let us first look at Mars and Eros.

Mars and Eros: The Drive of the Complex

The Oedipus myth is based on slaying and sexuality—slaying the man who turns out to be his father, and loving the woman who turns out to be his mother. The nature of the unconscious complex is of course such that only after the deed does he (or we) realize what has happened—the after-thought of Epimetheus rather than the forethinking of his brother Prometheus. Slaying and sexuality make up the fundamental pair of life principles, Mars and Eros, aggression and relatedness.

Mars, the warrior, who might kill, must not be confused with Thanatos, the death instinct, the inherent striving of everything living, says Freud, to "become inorganic once again" and to die "for *internal* reasons."[130]

In fact, according to legend, Sisyphus had overpowered Thanatos, so that no one died on earth anymore.[131] Maybe only a Sisyphus, hanging on to a meaningless life of repetition-compulsion, can outdo and take the wind out of death (and thus, the passion out of life as well). Fortunately, however, Ares (Mars) brought Death (Thanatos) back into life.

Eros and Thanatos form a different dyad from Eros and Mars. Thanatos, though, is not absent from Oedipus' life story, which begins with his near-annihilation by the forces of death, when exposed to and unprotected from the instinctual and archetypal powers outside the city boundaries.

Freud speaks of Eros as the "instinct of life," and D.W. Winnicott calls aggression, Mars, the "force of life." They form a pair of primary opposites, essential to human survival. Aggression is necessary for the fight into existence, as well as for attaining separation and individuation, but without Eros one remains a brutal barbarian, barely human.

Eros, the life instinct, is the principle of unification. Freud says, "The aim of [Eros] is to establish ever greater unities and to preserve them thus—in short, to bind together."[132] The sexual act, behind which we find Eros, is based on the tension that causes the very union that enables the creation of life.

---

[130] *Beyond the Pleasure Principle,* SE 18, p. 38.
[131] See "Death's Messengers," in *The Complete Grimm's Fairy Tales,* pp. 718f.
[132] *An Outline of Psychoanalysis,* SE 23, p. 148.

Etymologically, aggression comes from *ad gradior*, meaning "I move forward." Mars is the principle of forward movement and separation. The neonate finds himself at the crossroads of not-being-into-being.[133] The very proximity to not-life constitutes a threat, with a consequent fear of annihilation. This is the fear of being devoured by the Great Mother, by the "world of the dead."[134] There is a *stillness* of not-life, and we may assume that the death instinct is partly deflected into aggression, which enables the child to pull away from the threat. The basic aggression may be found in the child's very first movements, thus Winnicott sees the origin of aggressiveness as "almost synonymous with activity,"[135] as the life force that ensures movement rather than stillness. We find the lack of adequate aggression in the eternal child, of whatever chronological age, unable to detach from *liebestod* (love-death) in the embrace of original wholeness. This is uroboric incest, of which Neumann says,

> The Great Mother takes the little child back into herself, and always over uroboric incest there stand the insignia of death, signifying final dissolution in union with the Mother.[136]

We may look at Oedipus' two characteristic energies, Eros and Mars, from three perspectives along the ego-Self axis.

Mother Self—Father Ego

Firstly, we may consider Eros, unity and mother as pertaining to the Self and the archetypal world, and Mars, differentiation and father, on the other hand, as pertaining to ego and consciousness. Neumann says it thus:

> In the history of humankind the differentiation of man and woman belongs among the earliest and most impressive projections of opposites. . . . For this reason every archetypal opposition easily assumes the symbolism of the Masculine and the Feminine, and hence the opposition of conscious and unconscious is experienced in terms of this symbol, the Masculine identified with consciousness and the Feminine with the unconscious.[137]

---

[133] See Shalit, *The Hero and His Shadow: Psychopolitical Aspects of Myth and Reality in Israel,* pp. 47ff.

[134] "Psychological Aspects of the Mother Archetype," *The Archetypes and the Collective Unconscious,* CW 9i, par. 158.

[135] "Aggression in Relation to Emotional Development," *Collected Papers,* p. 204.

[136] *The Origins and History of Consciousness,* p. 17.

[137] *The Fear of the Feminine,* p. 6.

Freud, while not referring to the archetypal layer, expresses an aspect of this view when elaborating the differences of the Oedipus complex as regards the boy and the girl. On one end of the complex, he writes, "the girl is driven out of her attachment to her mother," and at the other pole, as regards the boy, the complex is "abandoned, repressed and, in the most normal cases, entirely destroyed, and a severe superego is set up as its heir."[138] Relevant to our discussion is not the difference Freud outlines between the boy and the girl, but the movement of the Oedipus complex along an axis from attachment to superego.

The Self is the central, unifying principle in one's psyche. Prior to the ego's separation from the Self, it holds "the innate, archetypal potentials that may be given expression by a person."[139] Eli Weisstub identifies the Self with the feminine principle.[140] This is particularly pertinent as concerns the Self in its generative, creative, symbol-forming capacity. It is the divine spark that ignites the seed of life in the womb of the Great Mother. The Self is the archetypal symbol, the arche-symbol, or symbol of symbols, since its very essence, in Jungian terms, is *symbolos,* that is, union of opposites. Jung says that the symbols which are generated, and which we conceive of in consciousness as symbolic images, come to act "as *transformers,* their function being to convert libido from a 'lower' into a 'higher' form."[141]

In contrast to the basic healing energy of the Self's unifying symbols, the energy of consciousness arises from the tension between the opposites.

Legend has it that the Great Mother made a serpent from a ball of clay, which she rolled between her hands until it stretched into a snake.[142] From the ball, or *bolus,* of clay from which the serpent of the goddess is created, we trace the Latin name for the devil—*diabolos.* The New Testament refers to "that old serpent, called the devil and Satan."[143] The temptation of the serpent triggers the crime of consciousness—to taste the forbidden fruit of knowledge, of *dia-gnosis,* of knowing the one from the other. Whereas the *symbolos* ("throwing together") unites, the *diabolos*

---

[138] *Moses and Monotheism,* SE 23, p. 129.
[139] Samuels, Shorter and Plaut, *A Critical Dictionary of Jungian Analysis,* p. 136.
[140] "The Self as the Feminine Principle," pp. 425ff.
[141] *Symbols of Transformation,* CW 5, par. 344.
[142] See Barbara Walker, *Woman's Encyclopaedia of Myths and Secrets,* p. 232.
[143] Rev. 12:9; AV.

("throwing apart") separates, differentiates and splits. The devil does not allow man to rest peacefully in the paradisiacal embrace of the Great Mother. Rather, he awakens Mars, the aggressive energy, and forces man to draw the sword of knowledge, which in turn enables separation and differentiation.

Consequently, Eros and Mars form the necessary pair of libidinal regression and progression that enables a dynamic relationship between ego and Self. A meaningful ego-Self relationship constitutes the individuation process, which in the first half of life, or of analysis, pertains to the ego's separation and movement away from the Self.[144] This is the stage in which we deal with complexes.

The Primal Scene

Secondly, we may contemplate Eros and Mars solely in relation to the archetypal world from which the nascent ego has to germinate. Since the complex serves as path of transformation and transformative vessel from the archetypal to the human and personal, its task is twofold. It has to separate and produce distance, cutting-off from the archetypal, as well as uniting with it in order to bring something valuable therefrom. In order to evade the impact of the gigantic archetypal forces, the aggressive instinct must be strong enough. We may compare this to the depressive position of Melanie Klein, when the relation to the mother becomes one of ambivalence. The tie is no longer exclusively loving. Mother and Breast—the rounded breast with the nipple in its center, as primary symbol of the Self—become targets for aggression.

There is a need to attain the valuable energies and contents from the archetypal world. This is what comes to make up the archetypal core or nucleus of the complex. This is the undiluted archetypal spirit in the diluted matter of homeopathic medicine. Fusion and incest with the archetypal sphere achieve this. It can be compared with the ancient permission to have incest with the Great Mother, that is, the archetype, but not with the personal mother. This is the "mother-marrying" that "many a man has dreamt" of, that Jocasta relates to Oedipus.[145]

The primal scene is the archetypal image that Freud chose with great

---

[144] See Edward F. Edinger, *Ego and Archetype: Individuation and the Religious Function of the Psyche,* pp. 3ff.
[145] See below, p. 63.

intuition and wisdom as representing the need to elicit and extract love and aggression, the life principles, from their archetypal origins.

Contemplating the primal scene, Freud seems, most probably unintentionally, to have approached Jung's idea of the collective unconscious. Freud spoke of the primal scene, in which the child is supposed to have witnessed the parents having intercourse, as well as other primal fantasies (intrauterine existence, castration and seduction), as constituting a phylogenetically transmitted inheritance, and therefore as universal. J. Laplanche and J.B. Pontalis point at the significance "that these inaugural events are referred to as *scenes*, and that Freud attempted from the outset to identify a limited number of them as archetypal scenarios."[146]

Freud says:

> I believe these primal phantasies . . . are a phylogenetic endowment. In them the individual reaches beyond his own experience into primaeval experience . . . children in their phantasies are simply filling in the gaps in individual truth with prehistoric truth. I have repeatedly been led to suspect that the psychology of the neuroses has stored up in it more of the antiquities of human development than any other source.[147]

Laplanche and Pontalis recognize the great difficulty Freud's notion causes, since it indicates a substitution of seeking the etiology of neurosis in "circumstantial infantile traumas, in favour of a theory which . . . looked upon phantasy as the forerunner of the symptom."[148] This is the fundamental conflict between respective theories of trauma and complex.

Andrew Samuels emphasizes its significance, stating that "the primal scene has to do with origins and the mystery of a beginning," and it is "a creation and a symbol for life as it develops."[149] The primal scene entails the two opposing components of love and aggression. Its archetypal foundation is the parental union that enables the creation and coming-into-being (of the child itself), an image of togetherness and harmonious merger. However, it is also the image of paternal aggression against the mother that enables separation and forward movement.[150] The archetypal

---

[146] *The Language of Psychoanalysis*, p. 331.

[147] *Introductory Lectures on Psychoanalysis*, SE 16, p. 371.

[148] *The Language of Psychoanalysis*, p. 331.

[149] *The Father: Contemporary Jungian Perspectives*, p. 112.

[150] Paternal aggression refers here to the symbolic image and not to the concrete act, similar to Jung's symbolic treatment of incest.

image of the primal scene, as related to in the fantasies of the child, entails these two foundations, union and separation, in a *coniunctio oppositorum*, union of opposites, that forms the basis for development. The child takes hold of something, it commits the act of a Promethean theft, even stealing the very archetypal fantasy out of the parents' bedroom. But the child is also forced to leave something behind, as well as being left out, therefore experiencing the early feelings of abandonment that are inevitably linked to the child's very development.[151]

The Sword and the Shield

Thirdly, opposite the archetypal layer we find the ego and conscious identity, toward which the complex is heading. Here too, as the complex arrives at the city of the ego, martial and erotic energies are essential.

Mars is the warrior who identifies the other as enemy to be fought against, to be separated from, to project onto, and to repress (push back) into the shadow. Aggression is the force that establishes ego-boundaries and lies at the bottom of ego-strength and assertiveness. The hero's sword is the insignia of male ego-consciousness. But without Eros it becomes two-dimensional, aggressive, accusatory, rationalistic and unreflective.

The consequences of a one-sided ego are reflected in one man's dream, in which he finds himself

standing together with his two sons, at the verge of a cliff, looking down the abyss. A murderer with a gun appears, and says he has to push someone down the abyss. The dreamer has to choose, and unhesitatingly he chooses his sons, the *others*, to be pushed over the cliff.

The murderous complex has taken possession of the dreamer's ego. The danger of wounding (psychically, in this case) is imminent. In the absence of Eros and an integrated Mars, the dream-ego is unable to imagine the possibility of sacrificing itself, or of taking responsibility, turning toward the murderous complex and genuinely confronting it. All too easily he sacrifices the new, upcoming elements, his sons, whether as external objects or internal representations.

The Eros part of consciousness not only enables the experience of similarity and togetherness outwardly, relating to others, but is also accommodating for the unconscious, for the not-ego within. It makes the ego

---

[151] See "The Psychology of the Child Archetype," *The Archetypes and the Collective Unconscious*, CW 9i, par. 285.

reflective, moist, soulful, humble and less defensive.

The two Oedipal energies, Mars and Eros, enable a person both to get away from ("slay") the archetypal and bring something valuable therefrom. They enable the formation, the constellation, of ego both as separate and related, that is, as consciousness.[152] Aggression and relatedness are the instinctual energies by which the archetypal core or essence is driven to become human and personal; that is, they constitute the dynamic element of the complex. Oedipus possesses both these elements, Eros and Mars, but being an autonomous complex, he is no less in their possession, acting them out in a most disastrous way.

The Complex Path: From Archetype to Ego

In the story of Oedipus, as in many other hero myths, we find a dual set of parents, personal and archetypal.

Parents are often unconscious of the expectations and apprehensions that they bestow upon even their yet-unborn children. In this case the personal father, Laius, fears the new-born, whether we see Oedipus as his actual son or if we consider him intrapsychically as an upcoming new element, a complex, that moves toward its integration into the ego, as represented by Laius.

In the Oedipal drama, Thebes is the domain of the ego and the human sphere. Cadmus, a mortal man and not a god, was the founder of Cadmeia, the forerunner to the city of Thebes. He married Harmonia, the daughter of Ares and Aphrodite, that is, the principles of aggression and love, the prominent features of Oedipus. The gods participated in Cadmus' wedding, a rare favor granted an earth-born. Furthermore, Cadmus introduced the Phoenician alphabet to Greece. We can hardly imagine more profound expressions of a developing human consciousness than those we find in Cadmus. It seems reasonable to conclude that Thebes represents an advance in human consciousness.

Laius, king of Thebes, was a great-grandson of Cadmus. Psychologically, in myth and fairy tale, the king represents the dominant principle of collective consciousness.[153] Laius personifies its masculine aspects, such

---

[152] See Edward F. Edinger, *The Creation of Consciousness: Jung's Myth for Modern Man,* pp. 52ff, where consciousness is defined as "knowing with," meaning Logos with Eros.

[153] See von Franz, *The Interpretation of Fairy Tales,* p. 40.

as law, order, differentiation, separation, and aggression.[154]

Jocasta, the Queen, was, says Kerényi, "the source of royal power in Thebes, for in this city royal power corresponds to matrilinear relationships."[155] She plays a significant role in the kingdom. Her name means "Shining Moon," and we can take her to represent the feminine side of consciousness. That is, we find here the reflective, conscious side of the moon, pertaining to, for instance, Eros, relatedness and spiritual, feminine wisdom. In feminine consciousness, in contrast to masculine,

> the ego has more the task of directing the libido toward the observed life processes or events and intensifying them than that of abstracting from them and hence arriving at an extension of consciousness. Typical for this observing consciousness is the act of contemplation where energies are guided toward a content, process, or midpoint while the ego establishes a participation with the emotionally colored content and lets it impregnate and permeate it. This differs from the extremely patriarchal consciousness that distances and abstracts itself from the content.[156]

The moon, with its "characteristically feminine" quality, shines only in the darkness of the night, "after the light of the sun is removed and the masculine activities of the workaday world are laid aside," says M. Esther Harding.[157] Or, as Jung expressed it, "Yin is like a mother-of-pearl image hidden in the deepest recesses of the house."[158]

In Laius we find masculine aspects of consciousness, excessively relying on strict and stern ego-boundaries. A one-sided and repressive ego is

---

[154] There is of course no immediate, unmediated relationship between masculine and male or feminine and female. Samuels explores the relation between sex and gender, calling the assertion that men be expected to behave in a culturally defined masculine way, and women in a culturally defined feminine way, "simplistic in that they assume a *direct* equation between anatomy and psychology." *(The Father,* p. 19) Neumann similarly clarifies this when stating,

> "Masculine" and "feminine" are used here as symbolic terms and are not to be identified concretely with "man" or "woman" as the bearers of specific sexual characteristics. Man and woman are psychologically bisexual since in the unconscious both have contra-sexual "authorities," the anima in the man and animus-figures in the woman. *(The Fear of the Feminine,* p. 65, note 3)

Often it seems preferable to use yin and yang rather than feminine and masculine.
[155] "Oedipus: Two Essays," in Kerényi and Hillman, *Oedipus Variations,* p. 7.
[156] Neumann, *The Fear of the Feminine,* p. 105.
[157] *Woman's Mysteries,* p. 65.
[158] Ibid., quoted by Harding.

often haunted by neurotic fear evoked by the frightening messages sounded by the oracle residing in the unconscious. Such neurotic fear defensively excludes whatever arises from the depths of the unconscious, making use of phobic, compulsive and martial defenses to the detriment of Eros, affection and loyalty.

In Jocasta we find feminine consciousness, reflective light in the dark, willing to receive what emerges from the depths, listening to the dreams that swim in the nightly mirror of the moon-lit lake of the soul. This is a less differentiated, less aggressively defensive and more reflective aspect of consciousness. It is therefore more easily intruded upon, and sometimes drowns in dreams and magic, devoured by incest and complexes.

The Wounding of Oedipus

The dominant, ruling masculine principle of consciousness is threatened by a new upcoming element. Many fathers have son complexes, unable to accept the new instinctual energy of the younger generation.

Laius is scared to death by the foreboding that he hears from the depths of his unconscious. He therefore does what a defensive ego sometimes does—defends itself to death. He prevents the new-born Oedipus, the upcoming complex, from entering the sphere of the personal, from growing up in the city of Thebes. The complex is cruelly separated from the ego, ruthlessly left to its grim fate outside the protective confines of the city. It therefore becomes autonomous, the kind of complex that has us in its grip.

Laius does two prominent things, he wounds Oedipus and he exposes him. Transposed to parent-child interaction, the wounding is a neurotogenic defense, the exposure psychotogenic.

Initially, Laius wounds Oedipus in the foot. Besides Oedipus' distinctive energies, Mars and Eros, being wounded in the foot is his other pivotal characteristic. It is, moreover, closely related to his answer to the Sphinx's riddle.

Inasmuch as we deduce the essence of Prometheus from his name, the forethinker, we have reason to believe, as did Freud and Jung, that as regards Oedipus as well, his secret lies hidden in his name. His adoptive archetypal parents gave him his name, which means "Swollen Foot." We may safely assume that there is more to it than a purely medical observation of a physical symptom.

By wounding him, Laius makes Oedipus human. Everything human is wounded. To be human is to be wounded, crippled, mortal. Our complexes are our wounds, and our complexes cripple us, they wound us. When the complexes are too heavily defended against, they wound us more seriously. As humans, we are never complex-free. By wounding Oedipus, Laius makes him into a human complex, not only an archetypal energy, such as Mars or Eros.

Laius wounds Oedipus in the foot so that he cannot tread easily or stand firmly on the ground. He is not well rooted, and his connection with ego and reality is unstable. And yet, if we turn to Freud, the swollen foot of Oedipus is the swollen, erect penis (as he tells Jung in a letter written November 21, 1909).[159] Jung seems to have sensed this ambiguity, as reflected in his brief reference to Oedipus' name:

> The foot, as the organ nearest the earth, represents in dreams the relation to earthly reality and often has a generative or phallic significance. The name Oedipus, 'Swell-foot,' is suspicious in this respect.[160]

In other words, earthly, human potency and capability are not invincible and godlike, but are intertwined with and rely on our woundedness. As expressed in the *Tao-te Ching,* "The stiff and unbending is the disciple of death. The gentle and yielding is the disciple of life. . . .The hard and strong will fall. The soft and weak will overcome."[161]

The complexes inhabit the shadow, and without the instinctual excitation that roars in the shadow there is no human potency.

Additionally, Laius exposes Oedipus to nature, throws him into a deadly fate by unprotected and defenseless exposure to archetypal forces. Moreover, with his foot wounded, his developing ego cannot easily gain a firm hold on the ground, and would have needed particular parental attention, for instance a mother who compensates for the wounding father. Unprotected exposure kills or causes psychosis. It is the task of the personal parents to protect the child from the unmediated and too powerful intrusion from the world of archetypes. Psychotogenic, psychosis-inducing parents don't manage to do this. (As concerns certain children, it sometimes seems impossible to protect them from becoming psychotic.) The unprotected exposure to Mother Nature makes her overwhelming and dangerous, and the wild animal soul drives us mad or kills us.

---

[159] *The Freud/Jung Letters,* p. 266.
[160] *Symbols of Transformation,* CW 5, par. 356.
[161] Lao Tsu, *Tao-te Ching,* chap. 76 (not paginated).

One adult patient, for instance, who lost her mother at an early age, often roamed the streets as a young child, alone, with no way to get into her home. She frequently dreamed, compensatorily, that she slept peacefully in her bed while her parents stood outside on the balcony, between her room and the sea, protecting her from huge threatening waves roaring in from the ocean.

We find extreme cases of exposure for instance among individuals who have been exposed to early parental loss, with no adequate alternate caregiver, and in people who have experienced childhood abuse or other early trauma, such as war, terror or the Holocaust.

Internally, it is the task of the complex to dismember the archetype, preventing it from overwhelming the developing child, enabling the archetypal core to have a valid but not devastating impact on the person. Complexes become autonomous due to the ego's defensive attitude, preventing the complex from entering the realm of the ego and conscious identity. Not the *content* of the complex but the *autonomous strength* it gathers in the shadow makes it pathological.

Oedipus' Journey

Oedipus is raised by his adoptive, archetypal parents in Corinth.[162] King Polybus is an offspring of the god Hermes. However, Oedipus is told that he is not a true son of the mild-hearted king. That is, he is not fully archetypal. This realization sets Oedipus going. He can no longer stay in his father's house, in the realm of the archetypal. He leaves for Delphi to inquire of the oracle, who has the feminine wisdom of the unconscious that can tell you where you come from and what your fate will be. This is the substance that mediums and fortune-tellers are made of. This is the "medial woman" who, says Toni Wolff, "is immersed in the psychic atmosphere of her environment and the spirit of her period, but above all in the collective, impersonal, unconscious."[163]

Laius has, in the meantime, also started out on his journey to ask the oracle at Delphi how to rid Thebes of the Sphinx.

The Sphinx had arrived at Thebes to punish Laius, either for having abducted the boy Chrysippus because of his beauty, or for having exposed Oedipus. Both explanations seem to point in the same psychological di-

---

[162] See, for instance, Robert Stein, *Incest and Human Love,* p. 67.
[163] "Structural Forms of the Feminine Psyche," p. 9.

rection. The Sphinx, the negative and destructive female element from the unconscious, had arrived in the city, endangering the ego, because of Laius' incapacity to integrate the Oedipus complex, the threatening elements of aggression and union that form the drive for development and maturation. He had preferred the childlike beauty of innocence, Chrysippus, who was later either murdered or committed suicide. That is, while narcissism reaches its archetypal peak at age sixteen (the age at which Narcissus drowns in his own image), the beauty of childhood innocence comes to an end even earlier. An ego excessively enchanted by them cannot integrate more complex elements into its conscious identity. Such an ego remains immature, sometimes in spite of an external appearance, a persona of kingly rule, for instance the CEO who is caught seducing the messenger boy (or girl), the priest who exploits his godlike persona, and so on. The result is that monstrous and destructive aspects of the unconscious intrude upon and possibly devour the ego. Jung makes this unambiguously evident as he traces the genealogy of the Sphinx. He writes:

> She was a daughter of Echidna, a monster with the top half of a beautiful maiden, and a hideous serpent below. This double being corresponds to the mother-imago: above, the lovely and attractive human half; below, the horrible animal half, changed into a fear-animal by the incest prohibition. Echidna was born of the All-Mother, Mother Earth, Gaia, who conceived her with Tartarus, the personification of the underworld. Echidna herself was the mother of all terrors, of the Chimera, Scylla, the Gorgon, of frightful Cerberus, of the Nemean lion, and of the eagle that devoured the liver of Prometheus. She also gave birth to a number of dragons. One of her sons was Orthrus, the dog of the monster Geryon, who was slain by Heracles. With this dog, her own son, Echidna incestuously begat the Sphinx. This should be sufficient to characterize the complex whose symbol is the Sphinx. It is evident that a factor of such magnitude cannot be disposed of by solving a childish riddle. The riddle was, in fact, the trap which the Sphinx laid for the unwary wanderer.[164]

In Delphi Oedipus is told the fateful truth by Pythia, the female seer in the unconscious.

The oracle in Delphi originally belonged to Gaia, the Earth, who turned it over to Themis, her daughter, who also was an earth-goddess, and from whom Apollo received or forcefully took hold of the oracle. In order to lay

---

[164] *Symbols of Transformation,* CW 5, par. 265.

claim to it, Apollo had to kill the guardian of the oracle and the earth-shrine, the female dragon-like serpent Python. The powers of Python survived in Pytho, the alternate name of Delphi, and in Pythia, the prophetess, who tells Oedipus of his fate.

Those seeking the advice of the oracle first had to pay a sum of money, then sacrifice, often a goat, to the gods, before setting foot in the temple of Apollo. Prior to entering the temple to pronounce her obscure prophecies, Pythia purified herself in spring water. In the temple she chewed on laurel leaves, sacred to Apollo, maybe thus inducing a state of trance.

Pythia was an old woman. She sat near the stone *omphalos,* the midpoint or navel of Gaia, the Earth Mother. She was seated in the *adyton,* an inaccessible underground chamber, which only she was allowed to enter. There she sat on the tripod, the bronze altar, uttering her oracular proclamations, which were then interpreted by the priest.

Sometimes we may have the most terrible impulses, making us act blindly, in despair and without thinking. This raw truth from the unconscious may lead us to be overtaken by affect, a sign that we are in the grip of a complex. As Kerényi says, "How often one races into the horrible out of fear for the horrible!"[165]

Complexes are often constellated by our urge to avoid them. This is the paradox of the messenger in *King Oedipus,* who brings the good news, which turns out to be very bad news, that Oedipus shall not fear the oracle's warning about patricide and incest, for King Polybus and Queen Periboea are not his parents. In fact, since his complex had its inflaming affect on Oedipus, he did not keep in mind that he had turned to the oracle, because he might *not* be their son. It lies in the character of an autonomous complex, residing outside of and in competition with the ego, not to be consciously differentiated, confused as regards its relationship to the personal as well as the archetypal. Robert Stein says it thus,

> The fact that Oedipus believed his substitute parents to be his real parents points to a lack of conscious differentiation between the personal and archetypal parents. While the incest taboo functions to prevent concrete incest, it serves to promote symbolic or spiritual incest with the mother substitute. Oedipus' unconsciousness, therefore, causes him to cut off from his substitute parents (the archetypal pair of opposites united in the image of the Royal Marriage or *hierosgamos*), out of fear of violating the incest prohibi-

---

[165] "Oedipus: Two Essays," in Kerényi and Hillman, *Odeipus Variations,* p. 12.

tion. As a consequence there is no possibility of Oedipus finding fulfillment of his incestuous longings, except concretely.[166]

If he had been less complexed, he would have kept the question about his identity in mind and not acted it out, even given Pythia's blunt behavior. However, had he returned to a tranquil existence in Corinth, developing in the usual way, avoiding his tragic fate, he would not have been the hero and somebody else would have had to carry the myth.

There are therapists that seem to find particular pleasure in telling their patients truths that they are not ready for, without respect for necessary defenses. In one such case the therapist of a twelve-year-old boy provocatively asked the mother, at their first meeting and without initially inquiring about her history, "Are you really the mother of this little boy?" He had cynically referred to this woman's overprotective attitude toward her only child. However, the therapist had not taken the mother's anamnesis, was unaware that she had spent her early years in different children's homes, and that her husband had been unwilling to have children until they were forty years old.

If Oedipus had not been in the grip of his own complex, a dialogue could have ensued for him to understand that it is the unconscious, his archetypal parents, the omnipotent parents of early childhood, that paradoxically have to be both slain as well as fused with. Instead, like the autonomous complex he is, he sets forth on his journey of acting out, so typical of someone like Oedipus, whom we know was easily enraged and now also overcome by the horror of his predicted fate.

From Delphi to Thebes

Incited by Pythia, Oedipus sets out from Delphi to Thebes, in the natural direction of the complex from the unconscious toward the realm of ego-consciousness and personal identity. But we must keep in mind that this complex is not going to be adequately integrated. He is oversensitive, impulsive, driven by dread and flooded by affect, which is characteristic of the autonomous complex. At a crossroad he meets Laius, who is trying to bring order to Thebes by getting rid of the raging monster, the Sphinx, that has settled in the vicinity of the ego, devouring the Thebans, the actual persons. However, Oedipus the complex stands in the way of the king, the ego, the ruling principle.

---

[166] *Incest and Human Love*, p. 67.

The ego is obviously on the right path, searching inward for answers to his pain and suffering. Laius has a unique opportunity when hindered at the crossroads. It is in the instances of threat, when one's road has been blocked, for instance by the conflicting encounter with a complex, when one feels the loss of meaning, when one has come to a crossroads, that one stands a chance of becoming conscious by finding a sense of meaning. This is Satan in his original connotation as adversary. "The primal meaning of the verb *satan* is *persecution by hindering free forward movement,*" says Rivkah Shärf Kluger.[167] This, notes James Hillman, is "fundamental to consciousness, which arises from tension."[168]

Patricide at the Cleft Way Crossroad

This is the *peripeteia,* the turning point of the drama. How do they act when encountering each other, ego and complex, Laius and Oedipus? The complex is provocative, stubborn and easily enraged; the ego is rigid and wants its way. The ego demands the complex step aside. A too rigid ego will often evoke, and thus encounter, uncontrolled and impersonal aggression. Laius falls victim to the very problem he sets out to solve, not understanding that the encounter at the crossroads provides him with a possibility to find a new way. The breakdown in Thebes, says Stein,

> could be related to a neglect and devaluation of the feminine principle . . .
> Thus the young men must be sacrificed to the Earth Mother until the feminine mysteries are re-activated and re-integrated.[169]

At the crucial crossroads Laius does not pay due respect to Hecate, another aspect of the dark feminine. He remains an overly masculine ego, according to which the king remains the ruler, even if his country is on the verge of collapse. Therefore, in fact, he activates the complex.

Oedipus' constitution compounds the two life instincts, Eros and Mars, but they are not integrated. His Eros is not one of virtuous feeling, relatedness and dialogue, but acted out as fusion and incest. His Mars is sheer and savage rage, not one of conscious differentiation and integrated assertiveness.

Oedipus says that he knows "no betters than the gods and his parents."

---

[167] *Satan in the Old Testament,* p. 29.
[168] Ibid., p. x.
[169] *Incest and Human Love,* p. 69.

That is, he is still trapped in an archetypal image of his parents. They still carry the omnipotent parental idealizations of early childhood. In fact, the entire drama at the Cleft Way Crossroad takes place on archetypal rather than human ground, as is evident, for instance, from this description:

> At this point the pass, shut in on either hand by lofty and precipitous mountains, presents one of the wildest and grandest scenes in all Greece; the towering cliffs of Parnassus on the northern side of the valley are truly sublime. Not a trace of human habitation is to be seen.[170]

For a child to develop satisfactorily, the killing and incest, aggression and fusion, that are the principal ingredients of the Oedipus complex, should be directed initially toward the archetypal and not to the personal. For the child not to be overwhelmed, it is the archetypal level that has to be "killed." We do this, for instance, when saying. "It was just a dream, a nightmare," or when telling a child that the hole in the bathtub is not the Great Mother's devouring mouth, or the entrance to hell.

It is, likewise, the archetypal that has to be "incestuously" fused with for the individual not to become alienated, concretistic and ego-defensive. This is accomplished by, for instance, remembering one's dreams, by playing for the sake of playing, or, for the three-year-old warrior on life's battlefield, withdrawal to the safe haven of the kitchen or mother's breast.

This is the incest referred to when in matrilineal society incest was something deeply desired, forbidden as regards the mortal mother yet permitted in relation to the divine primordial-mother, that is, in connection with the archetype. Even in *Oedipus Rex,* we hear Jocasta tell Oedipus, "Nor need this mother-marrying frighten you; many a man has dreamt as much."[171] That is, the female side of the ego knows this common theme, but one dreamed of and not to be acted out.

However, when the complex is autonomous and unintegrated, it strikes at the ego and the personal level. It becomes acted out. The actual father is rejected, slain, or, conversely, adulated and sexualized; the mother is overly attached to, or abandoned in panic. Murder and incest are acted out, as in the case of Oedipus. Oedipus does not intend to kill his father Laius or marry his mother Jocasta. He in fact tries to escape fate, running away

---

[170] James G. Frazer, note 4 to par. 3.5.7, in Apollodorus, *Apollodorus: The Library.*
[171] Sophocles, *The Theban Plays,* p. 52.

from the archetypal to the personal. But without adequately relating to the ego, the autonomous complex cannot hold a dialogue with its own archetypal core that has given the complex its meaning. It therefore acts in blind fate, and the life force of Mars, aggression, and the life instinct of Eros, relatedness, become destructive. Both are necessary for a human, personal existence. Together they constitute, as well, the dynamic ingredients of the complex as a vehicle for transforming the archetypal into the personal. But when the complex is autonomous and gathers competitive strength in the unconscious, the very life principles come to destroy the ego.

Oedipus acts like an autonomous complex, out of unconsciousness. He is blind long before he blinds himself. He lacks "ego-vision."

The Riddle of the Sphinx

Having slain Laius, Oedipus now has an open road to Thebes. From having been a somewhat troubled complex, he was fuelled by the fire of fear and horror by the utterances of Pythia. Encountering Laius, he turned into an ego-rejected, autonomous complex. Even worse, the masculine side of the ego was destroyed in the violent encounter. There is now hardly anything to block his rushing into the realm of the ego and fusing with the feminine side of consciousness. While the actual assimilation of a complex into consciousness is, essentially, desirable—and such is partly the case with Oedipus as well—the basic premise must be that it is the ego that allows the complex to enter. The ego controls the gates to the city. If a cardinal component of the ego has been killed, the complex will disastrously come to take possession of the remaining part.

We know that Laius set out on an heroic journey to consult with the unconscious in order to get rid of the Sphinx. This female monster has taken possession of the ego. The task now becomes that of Oedipus. Let us keep in mind that complexes are what make us human. So this is in fact what Oedipus makes use of in his encounter with the Sphinx.

There have been different psychoanalytic interpretations of Oedipus' answer to the Sphinx's riddle. Jung, perhaps not all too surprisingly, is not overly impressed with Oedipus, the complex that stands out as the archetypal passage to maturity in Freudian thinking. Jung writes,

> Oedipus [thought] he had overcome the Sphinx sent by the mother-goddess merely because he had solved her childishly simple riddle . . . . Little did he know that the riddle of the Sphinx can never be solved merely by the wit of man. . . .

. . . . The riddle was, in fact, the trap which the Sphinx laid for the unwary wanderer. Overestimating his intellect in a typically masculine way, Oedipus walked right into it.[172]

Freud takes the Sphinx question to mean, "From where does the child come?"[173] This might, particularly, have been Freud's riddle. As a matter of fact, no less does the Sphinx ask, "Where does man go?" The riddle proposes an exploration of man's life cycle as childhood, adulthood and old age. Thus, the essence of Oedipus' answer might be taken to mean that *man is mortal,* unlike the gods, and his life-span is limited. Ego is not Self, and the personal is not archetypal.

In Sophocles' *Oedipus the King,* the priest turns to Oedipus, recalling how he had broken their bondage "to the vile Enchantress," that is, the Sphinx, thus "it is not as holding you the equal of gods, but as the first of men, whether in the ordinary business of mortal life, or in the encounters of man with more than man."[174]

Oedipus is the embodiment of the human complex, the path upon which the two life forces—aggression and relatedness, separation and union—travel, whereby archetypal patterns are transformed into personal complexity, the divine into human. This is the paradoxical potency of complexes. While Oedipus is crippled, dragging along on his injured leg, the same swollen foot carries, as well, the potency of the erect penis. This is what paradoxically enables and destroys conscious human life.

Oedipus says,

> Born thus, I ask to be no other man
> Than that I am, and *will know who I am.*[175]

And he adds, "My sisters are the Seasons." One goes through a life cycle, grows up and grows old, passing through the season's of one's life.[176] This seems to be the heroic virtue of Oedipus' answer. The living individual is not an archetype, an ageless god, but mortal. So what kills the terrible man-eating monster seems to be the awareness of one's existential condition, with a beginning, a peak and an end, where the best one can do

---

[172] *Symbols of Transformation,* CW 5, pars. 264f.
[173] *Introductory Lectures on Psychoanalysis,* SE 16, p. 318.
[174] *The Theban Plays,* p. 26.
[175] Ibid., p. 55 (italics in original).
[176] See Daniel Levinson, *The Seasons of a Man's Life.*

is carry the spark of the divine, potentiated and enabled by lameness.

The Cancerous Complex

However, the ego of Thebes had been severely weakened by the fatal encounter at the Cleft Way Crossroads. The ego is inconceivable without its discriminatory aspect that, for better as well as for worse, divides and differentiates, defends and splits off. Laius, who had tried to defend Thebes by banishing Oedipus from the "ego-state," exposing him to the archetypal forces of the cold and dark night, had lost the battle and was now gone himself. Therefore, Thebes was all too impressed (see Jung's view, quoted above) and easily overtaken by the inflated, power-driven and immature, autonomous complex. As Stein says, Oedipus "has simply replaced the old king, but there has been no renewal."[177]

The result is that what should take place at the symbolic level becomes acted out concretely; now incest, like the previous patricide. The reflective side of the ego, Jocasta, does not banish into exile the complex that comes forth from afar. Rather, she welcomes the powerful young complex, embracing him. The shadows of powerful complexes are mirrored, reflected in the light of the shining moon, Jocasta, who is loyal to the forces of night and sleep rather than to the kingly rule of daytime, whose dominion ends as night falls, when he is overcome by wine and passion.

However, when a complex rules the ego, we are ill. In Oedipus' words,

> Sick as you all are, no one among you
> Is sick as I.[178]

The plague comes. An ego overtaken by a complex is easy to imagine —constantly inferior, enraged, helpless, childish, seductive, power-driven, or the like. The young mother, for instance, who thought she had ridden herself of her aggressive mother complex, finds herself in daily fits of rage against her own children, repeating her mother's very accusations. Or, the slim and well-groomed model, whose suppressed "fat-and-sloppy child" complex haunts her, reminding her of the child she once was and wants to forget, surfaces whenever she becomes intimate with a man, preventing her from forming a mature relationship.

---

[177] *Incest and Human Love*, p. 70.
[178] Kerényi, "Oedipus: Two Essays," in Kerényi and Hillman, *Odeipus Variations*, p. 20.

However, recognizing one's sickness, the shadow that has taken possession of one's ego, may enable the inward vision. Oedipus turns to the blind seer Teiresias to find Laius' killer. Well aware and respectful of the horror, Teiresias does not want to disclose the truth. Oedipus, who is a raging complex that has settled in the "ego-state," having taken over conscious identity, relentlessly insists on hearing it. He demands to know at any cost. When he and his deeds are identified, the remaining part of the ego is devastated, and Jocasta hangs herself. Then King Oedipus commits his final act of self-castration, jabbing out his own eyes.

The kingdom of the ego is lost when Oedipus knows who he is, just as youthful Narcissus must die when he comes to know himself, as Teiresias predicted. The truth has been thrown upon him, rather than gained through self-reflection. Therefore Oedipus will always tend to blame predestined fate, never himself, with the certitude and persuasion possessed only by a genuine complex:

> A stream of vile abuse—of murder and incest
> . . . .
> The gods so willed it—doubtless an ancient grudge
> Against our house. *My* life was innocent,
> Search as you will, of any guilty secret
> For which this error could have been the punishment,
> This sin that damned myself and all my blood.
>   Or tell me: if my father was foredoomed
> By the voice of heaven to die by his own son's hand,
> How can you justly cast it against *me*,
> Who was still unborn when the decree was spoken?[179]

---

[179] Sophocles, *Oedipus at Colonus*, in *The Theban Plays*, p. 101 (italics in original).

4
The Complex in the Shadow

The Autonomous Complex

The fundamental task of the complex is to serve as vehicle and vessel of transformation, whereby the archetypal essence is brought into living reality. The complex brings archetypal core and personal experience to bear on each other, uniting them in the flow of psychic life. It is in the healthy condition that the complexes enable a relatively smooth transition from the archetypal to the personal. However, the natural process of the complex may be disrupted for a variety of reasons, external or internal.

The archetype is fleshed out by real life. Only by the actual experience of, say, love, does the archetype come alive. If it weren't for the busy workings of the complexes in the layers of the personal unconscious, from its interface with the collective, archetypal unconscious and toward the boundaries of the ego, the archetype would either remain dormant or, worse, inundate the ego. In the first instance we find people who seem to be without a *joie de vivre,* dull and spiritless, schizoid or asthenic. We find the latter condition, where the archetypal world has inundated the person's sense of identity, in full-blown psychoses.

In "The Psychological Foundations of Belief in Spirits," Jung compares the experience of complexes with the primitive belief in souls and spirits: "Souls correspond to the autonomous complexes of the personal unconscious, and spirits to those of the collective unconscious,"[180] and makes an important distinction between soul complexes and spirit complexes:

> Whilst spirits are felt to be strange and as not belonging to the ego, this is not true of the soul or souls. The primitive feels the proximity or the influence of a spirit as something uncanny or dangerous, and is greatly relieved when the spirit is banished. Conversely, he feels the loss of a soul as if it were a sickness; indeed, he often attributes serious physical diseases to loss of soul.[181]

---

[180] *The Structure and Dynamics of the Psyche,* CW 8, par. 591.
[181] Ibid., par. 586. It should be noted, as does Jung's translator, that the translation from German of *Geist* (spirit) and *Seele* (soul) is not unproblematic. (Ibid., p. 300)

Jung then says that the soul complexes "belong to the ego and the loss of them appears pathological."[182] These are the complexes that rightfully should gain entrance and be assimilated into consciousness and the person's sense of identity. In the case of the so-called spirit complexes, the archetypal kernel is too strongly charged, and its association with the ego may mark "the onset of many mental illnesses."[183]

In psychoses, the archetypal world is too powerful and the ego too weak. The vessel of the complex has shattered, and cannot perform its transformative task. The ocean floods in and inundates the small strip of land on which the frail ego stands, or the ground shakes, reminiscent of the child's annihilatory fears. Dreams of earthquakes, a house on fire, or huge waves towering up from the ocean to forcefully crash onto the rocks, are examples of archetypal threats (though as dream images they are of course not psychotic). The complex may then invade the ego, as it did when Oedipus became king of Thebes.

> A fifty-five-year-old woman had always, including the eight years of her husband's illness and eventual death, considered herself to be "the lord and lady" in her house, by which she meant she coped with whatever hardships life exposed her to. Ever since childhood she had learned to withhold feelings of helplessness and fears of death. She took great pride in always being able to cope. She was greatly shaken by an earthquake in November 1995, a year and a half after her husband's death. She felt it was God's punishment for the assassination of Prime Minister Rabin (a not uncommon notion at the time), and she could no longer contain her feelings, overtaken by loneliness and incompetence. The repressed feelings of helplessness had constellated in the shadow, gathering momentum as complexes do in the backyard, now shaking the house and taking over its center, demanding conscious attention, causing pain in her heart, unbearable aches in her head and shaking legs.

In the healthy condition, the complex enables transformation; for instance, in place of a burned-down house grows a tree, and from the rupture in Mother Earth a bird takes flight. The autonomous complex carries no transformative charge, but is rather compulsive and obstructive.

The complexes transport the archetypes on the paths that lead through the dreams and the nightmares, the forests and the rivers, of the shadow-land of the personal unconscious. Likewise, the cluster of external object-

---

[182] Ibid., par. 587.
[183] Ibid., par. 590.

relations, perceptions and associations are drawn into the evolving complex. The manner in which experiences and objects are internalized depends upon their associations and connection with the inner, archetypal core of value and meaning. When there is no such connection, people and experiences will either pass by without being related to, unaccounted for, or they will flood in chaotically. In the first case we find a lack of affect, a sense of superficiality and meaninglessness; in the latter case identity-weakness and lack of will-power.

The complexes of the personal unconscious, in conjunction with the ego complex, are instrumental in the effective dialectic between ego and unconscious, and between ego and world. The adequately operating complex will enhance the ego—a person's sense of identity and belonging in the world. If the complex does not operate properly, either overloaded by its archetypal kernel, traumatized by experience or rejected by the ego, then the complex will take on a life of its own, becoming autonomous and pathological. Jung observes:

> The fact that [complexes] are painful is no proof of pathological disturbance. Suffering is not an illness; it is the normal counterpole to happiness. *A complex becomes pathological only when we think we have not got it.*[184]

That is, every complex must be considered in relation to the ego complex. Jolande Jacobi says that if the conscious mind does not understand, assimilate and integrate the complex, it becomes victim to the complex, "and is in greater or lesser degree engulfed by it."[185] Not every complex becomes fully integrated and assimilated into the ego. Yet, it only becomes pathological *if we think we have not got it*, whereby "the freedom of the ego comes to an end."[186] To know one's flaws and shortcomings, and to feel upset about them or embarrassed, is a step toward health, even though "awareness of a blind spot in the psyche [does] not preclude the development of unconscious effects, just as it [does] not guarantee the possibility of the ego's control of the complex."[187]

In other words, consciousness and the unconscious may be intertwined,

---

[184] "General Problems of Psychotherapy," *The Practice of Psychotherapy*, CW 16, par. 179 (italics added).
[185] *Complex/Archetype/Symbol*, p. 27.
[186] "A Review of the Complex Theory," *The Structure and Dynamics of the Psyche*, CW 8, par. 216.
[187] Liliane Frey-Rohn, *From Freud to Jung: A Comparative Study*, pp. 27f.

just as there may be various ratios of (un)consciousness, "from relative unconsciousness (as in parapraxes) to states of relative independence and autonomy . . . and on to those of definite possession."[188]

In the neuroses, we find the ego to be overly defensive. Avoidance, in the phobias, and defensive preoccupation in cases of obsession-compulsion, serve to ward off the upcoming complex, which threatens the rule of the ego. In a letter to Milena, his translator and friend, Franz Kafka writes, "I'm dirty, infinitely dirty, that's why I'm obsessed with cleanliness." And Milena, of a healthier breed, knowing that life is produced by the work of the shadow, responds wisely, "I don't see anything dirty, nothing of the kind, which provokes from the outside, only everything producing life from inside."[189] Freud says:

> We can say with certainty that what his [little Hans'] phobia disposed of were the two major impulses of the Oedipus complex—his aggressiveness towards his father and his over-fondness for his mother.[190]

That is, the ego sets up defenses lest its secure rule be threatened.

One woman felt threatened by electrical wires in her home, having delusions that they were like ominous snakes. She developed endless compulsive rituals of rearranging the wires/snakes into "harmless" patterns on the floor and the walls, and in her dreams she built defensive barriers of all too insufficient Lego-blocks against the threatening world of her instincts. Only during an extensive therapeutic process could she let go of her most severe defenses and accept the "electricity" of her instinctual life.

In provocative opposition to the ego's defensiveness, the impulses of the complex cause castration anxiety. ("Lest a horse should bite him, . . . bite off his genital, castrate him," as Freud says regarding Little Hans.)[191] When Freud claims that the castration complex lies at the foundation of the Oedipus complex, we can take this to mean that the genitality and vitality of the ego are threatened by the new instinctual (and archetypal) elements that arise from the unconscious. Yet, there is a perpetual duality to be kept in mind. The anxiety provoking threat of castration that the complex exerts on the ego may generate either neurotic defensiveness or

---

[188] Ibid., p. 27.
[189] David Z. Mairowitz and Robert Crumb, *Introducing Kafka,* p. 105.
[190] *Inhibitions, Symptoms and Anxiety,* SE 20, p. 107.
[191] Ibid., p. 108.

rejuvenating vital animal energy.[192] Little Hans' horse bite—or, in some dreams, being bitten in the leg by a dog, a cat or other animal—may mean being wounded by the complex that carries instinctual and archetypal energy. These symbolic castrations are like Oedipus' swollen foot, that is, they serve as potentiating wounds.

External events may, however, be too traumatic, breaking through ego-boundaries and defenses, as is the case for instance in child abuse. The traumatically caused autonomous complexes that constellate in abused children are not "potentiating wounds" but carry concrete scars, which divert energy from the ego and hamper development. In fact, as Janet had proposed, the autonomous complex sometimes constellated "as a defence against the anxiety caused by traumatic experiences."[193] And Jung clearly speaks about the *autonomous* complex when he says that they are "psychic fragments which have split off owing to traumatic influences or certain incompatible tendencies."[194]

A complex becomes autonomous when the ego rejects it, for example by splitting, denial or repression. When the ego prevents it from entering into consciousness, or expels it therefrom, the complex becomes pathological. Jung also refers to the autonomous complex when he says, "Everyone knows nowadays that people 'have complexes.' What is not so well known . . . is that complexes can *have us.*"[195]

As long as the complex is evolving out of its archetypal origin, developing toward consciousness, it is not pathological. The child who passes through the oral and anal phases is not orally or anally fixated. If, however, consciousness rejects the complex, drives it away from the home of conscious identity and dismisses it to the backyard of the shadow, it will gather autonomous strength and become provocative to the conscious ego complex. The following dream is an example:

> I am alone in my house. In the backyard there is a little limping puppy. She wants to get in, but I don't want to let her in; I am cold. Then I hear all kinds of dogs bark. I am afraid.

This dreamer was still too "cold" to turn toward the shadow in her

---

[192] See *Symbols of Transformation,* CW 5, par. 616.
[193] P. Everest, *The Multiple Self: Working with Dissociation and Trauma,* p. 447.
[194] "Psychological Factors in Human Behaviour," *The Structure and Dynamics of the Psyche,* CW 8, par. 253.
[195] "A Review of the Complex Theory," ibid., par. 200.

backyard, in order to relate to and let her "limping puppy" complex in. The puppy therefore grows into a pack of barking dogs, no less frightening to the dreamer than Hecate's ghostly hounds of hell.

The autonomous complex blocks the free flow of the ego and detracts energy from it. An inhibiting complex may be completely crippling to the ego. Whatever a person accomplishes in life is easily torn to pieces of worthlessness by a gnawing, self-rejecting inferiority complex.

Similar to the archetypes that dwell in the collective unconscious, the complexes operate in the shadow of the personal unconscious, which serves as an intermediary, transitional area between the collective unconscious and consciousness. Complexes, with their archetypal and instinctual core, travel back and forth, loading and unloading their freight.

There are complexes that bring new material into consciousness, giving archetypal structures human shape as persons and images that figure in our dreams, for instance finding a well in the desert, or being called out of the computer room high up in the building to meet the man with a basketful of vegetables. But there are also dream images whose main task it is to rid the ego of surplus material. These images, or personified complexes, make day-food into soul-garbage (the value of which should not be underestimated, for therein lie the treasures for the prospective hero to search out).

Such complex-images, then, enable us to pour some of our daily experiences, day-residues, into the bulk of subconscious knowledge, while others, like a sewage system, go further out into the sea of the unconscious. However, if we only dispose of our waste into the ocean, we create a psycho-ecological imbalance. Exploitation of the Self, as manifested by the sole use of the dream and the complexes that figure on its stage, to forget, deny and repress whatever is undesirable to one's conscious identity, causes gradual diminution and stiffening of the ego. As a result, the garbage pile might overflow, inundating the ego like a tidal wave, or threatening it as a horde of wild animals, nocturnal mice or barking dogs.

Particularly, we find the overload of the unconscious in posttraumatic dreams, where the traumatic event is reenacted night after night. The dream and the complexes try unsuccessfully to absorb the traumatic event and let it dissolve in the sea of the unconscious. Traumatic dreams are characteristically nonsymbolic, photographically repetitive of the traumatic event. It is as if the psyche tries to squeeze an experience of too great and harmful magnitude into the pipes of the sewage system, causing them to clog or crack. The traumatic event is then thrown back into consciousness wholesale, undigested, without the unconscious having been able to assimilate it.

A narrow, defensive, threatened ego will refuse the complexes entrance, deny their existence and repress their energy. Thus the complexes come to thrive and grow stronger in the darkness of the shadow. They cannot, then, travel their customary route from archetypal territory into the terra firma of the ego. Or, in Freud's words, this takes place when

> the censorship makes the normal connecting paths impassable. . . . We may picture, by way of analogy, a mountain region, where some general interruption of traffic (owing to floods, for instance) has blocked the main, major roads, but where communications are still maintained over inconvenient and steep footpaths normally used only by the hunter.[196]

Just imagine the truck drivers who have come from faraway lands, having had to travel over those "inconvenient and steep footpaths," now waiting outside the city gates of ego-consciousness to unload their diverse and complex merchandise, but not let in. They will soon grow impatient, irritated and angry. If unrelated to, they might possibly become violent, as the soul-food they are bringing is spoiled, having incubated for too long in the womb of the shadow.

The autonomous complex operates like "a kind of psychological magnet"[197] with a pair of one-colored glasses. Random experiences are drawn into its magnetic field and are tainted by the particular color of the complex, even if "objectively" they have little to do with it. A strong autonomous complex will attract whatever it encounters and draw it into its energy field, "just as a cancer cell begins to proliferate, 'devouring' the healthy cells."[198]

The impact of powerful complexes and their impingement on reality is striking in delusional (paranoid) disorders. In such cases the complex has split. One part, carrying the archetypal nucleus, for instance a sexual desire, is projected out, onto the external, persecutory object. The other part has taken possession of the ego, disrupting its capacity for judgment and discrimination. The complex-possessed ego becomes obsessed by feeling

---

[196] *The Interpretation of Dreams,* SE 5, p. 530.
[197] Frieda Fordham, *An Introduction to Jung's Psychology,* p. 22.
[198] Jacobi, *Complex/Archetype/Symbol,* p. 24.

persecuted by the split-off, projected part of the complex,[199] personified for instance as a sexually intrusive neighbor, or a secret agent sending messages through the TV or computer screen. Because it is split-off from the ego, the projection in paranoid conditions becomes like a persecutory spirit. And spirits, writes Jung, "viewed from the psychological angle, are unconscious autonomous complexes which appear as projections because they have no direct association with the ego."[200]

Freud speaks of repetition-compulsion as an autonomous factor. The autonomous complex, which noticeably pertains to "the Freudian aspect" of Jungian psychology, has precisely this repetitive-compulsive tendency, since it doesn't learn from experience, but rather paints experience in its own color. It possesses "the uncontrollable, compulsive character of all autonomous forces,"[201] and thus does not recline motionless in the psyche, but strives to gather more and more associations. A powerful autonomous complex becomes like the devouring monster in many a child's nightmare. Ego-defenses such as reaction-formation, sublimation, isolation and denial aim at dismantling the autonomy of the complex, at domesticating it so that it can be digested and assimilated into consciousness. Paradoxically, when applied appropriately rather than exaggeratedly in the child's development, ego-defenses are instrumental to the integration of complexes into the conscious personality.

However, when entrance into ego and consciousness is restricted, the complex starts acting like a splinter psyche. Jung notes:

> Dream psychology shows us as plainly as could be wished how complexes appear in personified form when there is no inhibiting consciousness to suppress them, exactly like the hobgoblins of folklore who go crashing round the house at night.[202]

In *Mysterium Coniunctionis* Jung draws further conclusions:

---

[199] See "The Psychological Foundations of Belief in Spirits," *The Structure and Dynamics of the Psyche,* CW 8, par. 584.

[200] Ibid., par. 585. In his footnote to this paragraph Jung says: "This should not be misconstrued as a metaphysical statement. The question of whether spirits exist *in themselves* is far from having been settled. Psychology is not concerned with things as they are 'in themselves,' but only what people think about them."

[201] Jacobi, *Complex/Archetype/Symbol,* p. 11.

[202] "A Review of the Complex Theory," *The Structure and Dynamics of the Psyche,* CW 8, par. 203.

The psyche is not a unity but a "constellation" consisting of other luminaries besides the sun. The ego-complex is not the only complex in the psyche. The possibility that unconscious complexes possess a certain luminosity, a kind of consciousness, cannot be dismissed out of hand, for they can easily give rise to something in the nature of secondary personalities, as psycho-pathological experience shows. But if this is possible, then an observation of the ego-complex from another standpoint somewhere in the same psyche is equally possible. . . . the critical portrayal of the ego-complex in dreams and in abnormal psychic states seems to be due to this.[203]

This is the ancient idea that "several souls can coexist in one and the same person,"[204] or, in Jung's words, "The primitive assertion that the individual has a plurality of souls is in agreement with our findings."[205] The luminaries or light-emitting souls or complexes, generated by the Self and driven by the instinctual forces of life, Mars and Eros, move through the darkness of the unconscious. Not every complex is destined for assimilation into consciousness, and others linger in the shadow for decades until they surface. Were they all to be made conscious, according to Freud's famous dictum, "Where id is, ego shall be," the instinctual vitality and driving force of the unconscious would cease. This is, fortunately, not possible, and more important is to respect the unconscious and the dynamics of the complexes. To respect the unconscious means to take another look.

Jung refers the constellation of complexes primarily to childhood. While they can constellate at any age, their developmental designation makes it evident that complexes pertain to the child. Since parents in many respects serve as mediators between the archetypal and the human world, by providing a good enough environment, complex psychology is closely related to parental attitudes, of which Jung says,

> The complex psychology of the child and in particular the psychic disorders of children are more often than not causally connected with the psychology of the parents, and in most cases one would do well to pay more attention to the faulty attitude of parents and educators than to the child's psyche, which in itself would function correctly if it were not disturbed by the harmful influence of the parents.[206]

---

[203] CW 14, par. 502.
[204] Jacobi, *Complex/Archetype/Symbol*, p. 12.
[205] *Mysterium Coniunctionis*, CW 14, par. 502n.
[206] "Foreword to the Hebrew Edition of Jung: 'Psychology and Education,' " *The Symbolic Life*, CW 18, par. 1824.

As in many other areas, for instance life-cycle research,[207] we see how Jung served as forerunner to ideas later cultivated by family therapists.

While many complexes constellate in childhood, they may surface at any age. For instance, a successful businesswoman suffers from a phobic fear of driving outside her neighborhood. The "little outsider girl" that she once was, whose parents could not afford the piano lessons that, in her complex-perception, *all* her friends took, who used to wait outside the teacher's house, keeps popping up. While she has crossed social borders, she is still restricted by the boundaries of her "little outsider girl" complex.

This woman's complex centers around the archetypal core of the child, and, more specifically, the archetypal images of the abandoned, rejected or orphaned child. Her childhood experiences have clustered around this archetypal image; what keeps them together as a complex is the feeling of helplessness and rejection.

The autonomous complex competes with the ego for accessible energy. A "good enough" mother is someone who can contain the process of dismemberment and de-integration, that is, the humanization of the archetypal images. This is likely to prevent the traumatization that comes from too drastic exposure to the archetypal world, on the one hand, and a too-sudden loss of "divinity," on the other. A good enough mother can also tolerate the humanization of the mother archetype itself, by which she, the mother, becomes less ideal and idealized, simply human. The child's mother-*imago* will then pass through the stages of change from omnipotence to impotence, and eventually competence.

However, a mother who identifies with the archetypal Good Mother will very likely encourage the formation of a positive mother complex. Her son may remain forever immature, never wanting to leave her, and, if forced away due to the demands of life, he might perpetually search for his mother's image in every woman who crosses his path.

On the other hand, a mother who enacts the Terrible Mother—mean, poisonous and devouring—may also inspire the formation of a positive mother complex. Her rejected daughter may want to please and tame her mother, and may compensatorily idealize her. She may search out similar kinds of women, in order to try to turn them into good fairies. Or, conversely, she may become a maiden desperately on the run, away from the

---

[207] Levinson, in *The Seasons of a Man's Life,* credits Jung as "the father of the modern study of adult development." (p. 4)

grip of her mother, only to repeatedly end up with female bosses that she experiences as aggressive and degrading mother-substitutes.

The complex becomes autonomous when the ego does not manage to integrate it into consciousness. That is, the complex that rises up from the unconscious and is not yet integrated into consciousness (and may never be) is not necessarily pathological, but if it encounters the ego, one's conscious identity, and is rejected, competes with, or engulfs the ego, the condition becomes pathological.

The Complex and the Call

The hero is someone who responds to a call to adventure.[208] Such calls are often dangerous, says Joseph Campbell,

> because they threaten the fabric of the security in which we have built ourselves and our family, . . . [yet] they carry keys that open the whole realm of the desired and feared adventure of the discovery of the self.[209]

The hero is that part of our consciousness that is willing to venture into the shadow to confront his or her own weaknesses and crippling wounds. Thus, by definition, the hero attends to the call, be it a challenge, the words of the oracle or an inner voice. Oedipus, for instance, sets off on his horrendous journey after hearing Pythia's pitiless words of horror that set his raging complex on fire.

Perseus, another Greek hero, is driven by devotion to his mother Danaë, determined to save her from King Polydectes, who wants to marry her against her will. He thus sets out on his journey in the netherworld, where he tames the Terrible Mother, decapitating the Medusa.

Perseus brings with him three essential features of the constructive, transformative complex.

First, from Athena he has received the shield, which protects him from looking directly at the Medusa, enabling him to see her through her reflection. Likewise, by means of the complex we see reflections of the archetype and are protected from direct and petrifying exposure. Archetypal exposure kills or drives us mad.

Second, Perseus wears the cap of invisibility. That is, he forgoes the need to wear a persona, the narcissistic need to be seen. This is essential

---

[208] *Hero with a Thousand Faces,* pp. 49ff.
[209] Ibid, p. 8.

when dealing honestly with our less-than-honorable complexes. To know ourselves, the Narcissus in us must die.

Third, he puts the decapitated head of the Medusa in a pouch that he throws over his shoulder. The complex serves as a container of the otherwise awesome exposure to the archetype. Thus, for instance, when he pulls the severed head of Medusa out of the pouch and holds it up to Polydectes and his astonished court, they all turn to stone. The shadow, Medusa, needs to be contained.[210] Just as complexes dwell in the shadow, the shadow is embodied in the complexes.

Symptoms and ill-being, depression and anxiety, alienation and crises stand in the way of familiar routine, yet they carry the keys. They force the sufferer to step off the highway, to go in search of a different route. The reluctant traveler, however, may prefer to barricade him- or herself behind phobic or obsessive-compulsive defenses, trying not to take notice of the call. Medical treatment, necessary when indicated, may kill the call. By deadening the pain, it can sometimes too easily be avoided. Some patients on Prozak claim they *know* that they are depressed, though they no longer *feel* it. This may reflect our present-day tendency toward fictitiousness and the "as-if" experience.

In analysis, we ascribe prognostic as well as diagnostic value to a patient's initial dreams. These dreams bring us the personifications of current and upcoming complexes that knock on the door to consciousness. In her initial dream a highly successful academician has to force her way out of a fortified building, together with her six-year-old daughter (in reality, she has none), to arrive at the shack, on the outskirts of town, of an old woman with long black hair and big breasts. She is "greater than life, like Mercedes Sosa." The dreamer is not sure if she can trust her and be protected, or if she must try to find her way back to the fortified building.

While outwardly successful, this woman had lost touch with aspects of her feminine self, both child and crone. She needed to force her way out of the comfort of defensive, intellectual ego-fortifications, to move toward "the outskirts of town," where we find peripheral people and newcomers to the city. She is willing to do this in the dream, which suggests that she will be able to endure upcoming complexes.

This is the beginning of her journey in therapy, in which she responds to the call to free herself and her inner child, her creativity and playful-

---

[210] See John Beebe, "Attitudes toward the Unconscious," pp. 12f.

ness, and encounter the Great Mother's protective as well as untrustworthy aspects. These three parts within her—creativity, ego and essential femininity—are not at peace with each other, and her task is to bring them into a livable relationship.

One man's call is expressed in this initial dream:

> He finds himself singing in front of his voice teacher, but out of tune. The teacher has not noticed yet, but the feeling of shame is imminent. He decides to set out on a journey. He finds himself in an unknown country, and comes to a small village in the mountains. In a narrow lane between the houses he meets a beggar, who ridicules him for singing out of tune, but at the same time presents the dreamer with an olive branch.

This man, a professional actor, needed to free himself from the false trappings of the persona, his "singing out of tune." Seeing his problem in this way made him intensely aware of being "out of tune" with himself. The persona complex had come to dominate his identity. External appearance and performance, not only in the theater, had come to carry greater weight than personal relations and an inner sense of meaning. The sense of falseness had started to gnaw on him, but only when depicted in the dream, the *out of tune* (complex) that interfered with his *singing* (ego), did he become attentive to what was rising from within. He could then attend to an inner voice, the Self, in the guise of a beggar (who wears no persona), and the branch of the tree that symbolizes the promise of new life, as it did after the flood in the Biblical story of Noah.

A young woman, mother of a ten-year-old son, herself with a negative mother complex, dreamed:

> There's a rumor that a baby lion has arrived in the neighborhood. Nobody seems to pay much attention to the rumor, maybe only I hear it. I feel I have to lure the lion into a cage and care for him.

The hero within, that part of the ego willing to attend to the call, hears the rumor that apparently is aimed at her, since others don't pay attention. This woman had great difficulty being attuned to more warm feelings, complaining of everyday arguments with her husband and son, as well as at work. Mars was considerably more prominent in her than Eros. However, after intensive work in therapy, the baby lion, a neglected complex, had arrived in the "neighborhood," that is, closer to the ego, indicating that she could now consciously care for it.

Jung refers to the lion as a libido symbol,[211] and to taming the lion as symbolizing the transformation of wrath into love.[212] The lion cub may reflect instinctual drives and passions, an inner potential for wisdom with feeling, that had previously been left "abandoned," and that the dreamer had to catch and care for, that is, consciously mother.

Feelings of anxiety and depression, as well as critical events, may serve as wake-up calls. As one allows images and symbols to approach consciousness, acknowledging projections, synchronistic experiences and the symbolic messages in dreams, the autonomous complex can be accessed. Realization is often painful, but indicates the beginning of healing.

The World Parents

Rina was thirty-two years old, married with two small daughters, when she came for therapy. While she seemed to function well in outer-life situations, she felt frustration and a growing sense of meaninglessness. She felt "emptied out," without "simple happiness" in her life. Along with her depression, she also felt a tremor of anxiety threatening to overtake her, to "push her over the cliff."

She lived with her family next to her parents in a village, just outside the small town where she had a part-time job as a graphic artist for a printer. Her younger and only sister had moved to the city at age twenty, soon after completing her army service. Rina was in constant contact with her parents, speaking to them several times a day. Together with her husband and daughters, they would have dinner at her parents' house every evening. After dinner, she would usually prefer to stay on, in spite of her husband's aggravation. When he would insist she come home, she called him selfish and inconsiderate.

Rina presented her parents as the perfect role model for a marital relationship. They formed an inseparable unit, always harmoniously in agreement and consulting with each other. Rina thought their symbiotic relationship was wonderful, and tried to enforce a similar one on her rather mildly protesting husband. She felt her parents knew best and did not question their authority, echoing Oedipus' remark that he knows "no betters than the gods and his parents." When she gave birth, both parents came to the hospital, and later instructed her in child-rearing practices.

---

[211] "The Concept of Ambivalence," *The Symbolic Life,* CW 18, par. 1078.
[212] *Psychology and Alchemy,* CW 12, par. 522.

Rina did not have the strength and confidence to commit the necessary acts of disobedience, separation and differentiation, to "slay" the parents, in order to become an autonomous and mature person. Her "great parents" remained a childhood idealization, a central complex, held on to at the price of her individual development and ability to take on a mature role in her own family.

Like every complex, Rina's parental complex has an archetypal core. We find it in the mythical image of the World Parents. James Frazer says:

> It is a common belief of primitive peoples that sky and earth were originally joined together, the sky either lying flat on the earth or being raised so little above it that there was not room between them for people to walk upright.[213]

The World Parents constitute the original pair of opposites that initially are not separated. In a Polynesian creation myth, for instance, we find Father Sky and Mother Earth in a nearly eternal, loving embrace.[214] The creatures born in the darkness between their united bodies could, however, no longer endure the suffocation, and held council what to do. Father of Human Beings suggested simply slaying the World Parents, but Father of the Forests suggested separating them by pushing them apart. Standing on his head (that is, an inverted tree), he pushed away Father Sky, and there was light. Von Franz points out how in the myths of separation of the World Parents, "emphasis is laid on the fact that space is needed, so that the whole of creation can come into existence between heaven and earth."[215] And she goes on to say:

> Unconsciousness, when outdated, has a suffocating effect upon the individual. Young people, for instance, speak of being suffocated at home. The unconscious identity with [the family] is at first all right, and is a kind of amniotic fluid in which the embryo swims around, but later it becomes suffocating and one begins to feel one cannot breathe and needs a wider space.[216]

The separation of the World Parents, writes Neumann, "the splitting off of opposites from unity, the creation of heaven and earth, above and below, day and night, light and darkness" is a "monstrous misdeed and a

---

[213] Quoted in Neumann, *The Origins and History of Consciousness*, p. 103.
[214] See Alexander Eliot, *The Universal Myths*, pp. 85f.
[215] *Creation Myths*, p. 239.
[216] Ibid., p. 243.

sin," marking the beginning of conscious human existence.[217] That is, ego development can take place only in so far as original unity is broken and the pair of original opposites separated. This is the exit from paradise, the breaking up of what Jung, following the anthropologist Lèvy-Brühl, calls *participation mystique*.[218] In this original state there is no separate identity; the ego is undifferentiated from the Self, and there are no ego-boundaries. This betokens a primitive mentality in which, writes Jung, "man has a minimum of self-awareness combined with a maximum of attachment to the object; hence the object can exercise a direct magical compulsion upon him."[219] We find this in cases of projective identification. Neumann:

> Differentiation of the ego, separation of the World Parents, and dismemberment of the primordial dragon set man free as a son and expose him to the light, and only then is he born as a personality with a stable ego.[220]

Rina's parental idealization was such that the ego identified with and was in the grip of the complex. While she functioned well in society, she was undifferentiated, without a firm sense of herself as a separate person. She adhered to the norms and conventions enforced by her parents, in many ways remaining a child rather than a grown-up. In this state of *participation mystique* there is no differentiation between I and You. The ego, as a separate and willful entity, has not yet been born.

In analysis she started to bring up repressed childhood memories, many of which concerned her need for self-expression. However, as she painfully recalled, she would be scolded and punished, for instance for not being dressed in the somewhat old-fashioned way her parents had insisted upon, in contrast to the much freer and casual ways of her school-mates. She recalled how both parents, together, used to spank her on her buttocks. She had thought of this as "their educational right," but now felt it to be sadistic and humiliating. As childhood memories kept emerging, with a feeling-tone different from that previously experienced, she dreamt:

> I am driving on a narrow road into the Negev Desert. In the middle of the desert is a house. It looks like my parents' house, but has no windows. The

---

[217] *The Origins and History of Consciousness*, p. 103.

[218] "Definitions," *Psychological Types*, CW 6, par. 781.

[219] "General Aspects of Dream Psychology," *The Structure and Dynamics of the Psyche*, CW 8, par. 516.

[220] *The Origins and History of Consciousness*, p. 106.

house is empty, I don't feel like being there. Two people sit on the floor, old
and ugly. Only after some time do I see that they are my parents. I ask for
water, I want to drink and have a shower, but they say there is no water.
There is a kind of well in the house, but I see it's empty.

She wondered, "Is this what my parents really look like?"—becoming
increasingly bewildered and upset, saying that she had "never looked at
them from the outside." She was increasingly aware of the repressed
shadow side of childhood. Her idealized image of her parents and childhood was replaced by the capacity to see them from a distance.

The image of imprisonment and the absence of water troubled her. It
was hard for her to accept the idea that her parents may not have the life-
giving resources she needed. However, for the well to connect with the
wisdom from below, the unconscious, it must come out of her parents'
house, down on the ground, even if on the surface the earth is dry and arid.
The well cannot serve as a life-giving womb of the Great Mother from
within her parental complex.

By releasing her painful pent up feelings, particularly in relation to her
mother, during the following months of therapy she was able to bring the
well to her own ground, however problematic. By confronting her shadow
and other complexes, she could eventually give birth to her ego and start
to care for herself. She then dreamed:

> Someone brings a little girl found in a park nearby. She is wounded. She
> looks terribly dirty and neglected. I bring her home to her parents, who live
> nearby, but they say it's not their child. I get very angry with them, but it
> doesn't help, and I wonder what will become of the little girl.

Associating to the dream Rina said, "The small child is me, lost, alone,
exposed to danger. Can it really be that those parents of the child in the
dream have something to do with my own parents, that it is not really *me*
they are interested in?"

The central image that emerges in the dream reflects how the broken
connection to the Self has been personified as a neglected child complex.
By appearing as a dream-image, the lost connection can be further dealt
with. Furthermore, this dream shows an important element of complex
psychology, namely that complexes are not rigid structures but dynamic
relationships. Jung writes:

> The complex has an abnormal autonomy in hysteria and a tendency to an
> active separate existence, which reduces and replaces the constellating

power of the ego-complex. . . .

A purposive treatment of hysteria must therefore strengthen what has remained of the normal ego, best achieved by introducing some new complex that liberates the ego from domination by the complex of the illness.[221]

Even if new complexes are usually not intentionally introduced in the course of analysis, we often find the replacement of one complex by another. It may be a question of symptom substitution, whereby one autonomous complex replaces another, or a healing process in which the working through of different layers of the soul frees up the vital movement in the shadow; or in Jung's words, a "new complex that liberates the ego from domination by the complex of the illness."

Thus, in Rina's case, when the ego started to deal with the great parents complex, the compensatory abandoned child complex emerged, the realization of which further helped her to establish a separate identity.

The Abandoned Child

The abandoned child that had been lost has now been found. A helpful "someone" has been awoken, a soul guide that can bring Rina into contact with her deeper wound, by bringing the lost child into consciousness. She had lost contact with her inner world, as represented by the wounded and neglected child. Having remained in immature identification with her parents, she had disowned and abandoned her self.

Abandonment distinctly reflects the difference between complex and trauma. As an actual event in childhood, being abandoned by a parent due to loss, abuse, violence or otherwise, inflicts a catastrophic wound (even if the person may be coping well in outer life). Not only physical, but emotional and psychological maltreatment as well, imply abandonment. Yet, though not every child has been exposed to the above kinds of trauma, everyone can, usually with ease, recognize feelings of abandonment, since it is an archetypal condition.

Dreams of an abandoned child are common, and mythology, fairy tales and literature are replete with the abandoned and orphaned child, from Moses to Oedipus and on to Oliver Twist. Abandonment is often a significant point of departure for the hero on his or her journey. It is a sign of waking up to the need to care for the child within. For example:

It's the end of the workday. I suddenly realize that I have forgotten a (my?)

---

[221] "Studies in Word Association," *Experimental Researches,* CW 2, pars. 861f.

small child at home. I drive as fast as I can, but the road is blocked. Road-work is going on. A worker takes me to the side of the road, into a little forest. In a hole in the ground I see the child. I want to call for a doctor, but can't wait any longer. I lean down and stretch out my hand, and with a lot of effort I finally manage to pull out the child. If I had come a little bit later, I don't know if it would have survived.

The woman who dreamed this has had to work hard in order to realize that she had forgotten her child (of undefined gender). It has been forgotten at home, within herself. However, the road is not easily accessible. She cannot rely solely on the familiar route of her conscious ego, but needs to look at the side of the road. Finally, she has to engage her own healing resources to revive the child.

Andersen's "Little Match Girl" is a heartbreaking picture of misery:

It was terribly cold; it snowed and was almost dark, the last evening of the year. In the cold and gloom a poor little girl, bare headed and barefoot, was walking through the streets. When she left her own house she certainly had had slippers, but of what use were they? They were very big slippers, and her mother had used them till then, so big were they. The little maid lost them as she slipped across the road, where two carriages were rattling by terribly fast. One slipper was not to be found again, and a boy had seized the other, and ran away with it. He thought he could use it very well as a cradle, some day when he had children of his own. So now the little girl went with her naked feet, which were quite red and blue with the cold. In an old apron she carried a number of matches, and a bundle of them in her hand. No one had bought anything of her all day, and no one had given her a farthing.

Shivering with cold and hunger she crept along, a picture of misery, poor little girl! The snow-flakes covered her long fair hair. In all the windows lights were shining, and there was a glorious smell of roast goose, for it was New Year's-eve.

In a corner formed by two houses, she sat down, cowering. She had drawn up her little feet, but she was still colder, and she did not dare to go home, for she had sold no matches, and did not bring a farthing of money. From her father she would certainly receive a beating, and besides it was cold at home, for they had nothing over them but a roof through which the wind whistled.

Her little hands were almost benumbed with the cold. Ah! A match might do her good, if she could only draw one from the bundle, and rub it against the wall, and warm her hands at it. She drew one out. R-r-atch! How it sputtered and burned! It was a warm bright flame, like a little candle, when she held her hands over it; it was a wonderful little light! It seemed to the little girl as if she sat before a great polished stove—how the fire burned! How comfortable it was! But the flame went out, the stove vanished, and she had only the remains of the burned match in her hand.

A second was rubbed against the wall. It burned up and light fell upon the wall, which became transparent like a thin veil, and she could see through it into the room. On the table a snow-white cloth was spread; upon it stood a shining dinner service; the roast goose smoked gloriously, stuffed with apples and dried plums. And more splendid—the goose hopped down from the dish, and waddled along the floor, with a knife and fork in its breast, to the little girl. Then the match went out, and only the thick, damp cold wall was before her. She lighted another match. Then she was sitting under a beautiful Christmas tree; it was greater than the one she had seen through the glass door at the rich merchant's. Thousands of candles burned upon the green branches. Then the match went out. The Christmas lights mounted higher. She saw them now as stars in the sky; one of them fell down, forming a long line of fire.

"Now some one is dying," thought the little girl, for her old grandmother, the only person who had loved her, and who was now dead, had told her that when a star fell down a soul mounted up to God.

She rubbed another match against the wall; it became bright, and in the brightness the old grandmother stood clear and shining, mild and lovely.

"Grandmother!" cried the child, "Oh! Take me with you! I know you will go when the match is burned out. You will vanish like the warm fire, the warm food, and the great glorious Christmas tree!"

And she hastily rubbed the whole bundle of matches, for she wished to hold her grandmother fast. And the matches burned with such a glow that it became brighter than in the middle of the day; grandmother had never been so large or so beautiful. She took the little girl in her arms, and both flew in brightness and joy above the earth, very, very high, and up there was neither cold, nor hunger, nor care—they were with God!

But in the corner, leaning against the wall, sat the poor little girl with red cheeks and smiling mouth, frozen to death on the last evening of the Old Year. The New Year's sun rose upon a little corpse! The child sat there, stiff and cold, with the matches of which one bundle was burned. "She wanted to warm herself," the people said. No one imagined what a beautiful thing she had seen, and in what glory she had gone in with her grandmother to the New Year's day.[222]

---

[222] Andersen, *The Complete Illustrated Works,* pp. 357ff. (slightly modified).

In this short tale, Andersen has drawn a powerful picture of agony and abandonment. One need not know the winter of the North to feel the shivering cold. Though the setting and the tone are very different, the little match girl's bare feet on the freezing ground are reminiscent of Jason and Oedipus. Jason, setting out on his heroic journey, sacrifices one sandal by carrying the mother goddess, Hera, across the river. Likewise, the little maid crossing the street is forced to sacrifice the slippers her mother had used—one of them to the little boy thief's motherly instincts. Her naked feet, "red and blue with the cold," resembling Oedipus' swollen foot, hamper her ability to face the harsh reality at the turn of the year.

The little match girl is an outsider. She is not part of the light, the warmth, the food and joy of being inside a home. This pertains to the early feelings of being thrust outside, separated from paradise, ejected from the protective and nurturing womb. However, to remain forever inside turns protection into prison, nourishment into poison. Vulnerability and loss are aspects of development. As Jung says:

> "Child" means something evolving towards independence. This it cannot do without detaching itself from its origins: abandonment is therefore a necessary condition, not just a concomitant symptom.[223]

Yet, the little match girl does not look for independence, but rather for a way out of abandonment and loneliness. She cannot rely on her personal parents; father beats her, mother takes her slippers, and the roof leaks. As in cases of actual abandonment, home is a cold place. Rather, she dreams of her Grand Mother, a variant of the Great Mother.

In cases of abandonment as a traumatically induced autonomous complex, there is often a compensatory search for protection. When, on the other hand, abandonment pertains to the psychological developmental process, as for instance at the onset of many hero-cycles, it is constellated by the need to sacrifice the reverie of dwelling in the safety and security of the divine.

A Mother Complex

The archetype of the Great Mother has both a generative, creative aspect, and a devouring, killing side (the Terrible Mother). She is the archetypal

---

[223] "The Psychology of the the Child Archetype," *The Archetypes and the Collective Unconscious,* CW 9i, par. 287.

Earth Mother who gives birth and creates, devours and kills. Etymologically there is a connection between mother (Latin *mater)* and matter. The Earth Mother is the womb from which life springs, but "life and birth are always bound up with death and destruction."[224] The womb of the earth from which life springs must be fertilized with sacrifices of the dead in order to bring forth further life, to again give birth. Mother Earth is both womb and grave, and her cycle is an endless one of birth-death-rebirth.

The collective unconscious, from which psychic life springs, can be represented by the image of the Great Mother, which is the archetypal idea of an entity that can give birth to the ego as well as devour it. This idea is externally represented, for instance, by the ocean from which islands and continents arise, upon which humans can then make the earth fertile and build cities. It is the great sea on which heroes venture, seamen sail off to bring merchandise from one culture to another and thus connect between them, and it is the unpredictable sea which may drown the sailor and shipwreck the hero.

In myth and fairy tale we find the Great Mother in her nurturing and embracing aspect as well as in her devouring, poisonous and murderous aspect. When she is terrible, the Great Mother evokes fears of annihilation. She may be the Baba Yaga witch or evil stepmother of fairy tales, or Kali in Indian mythology, dark and all-devouring, simultaneously giver of life and devourer of her children; and she is the Gorgon, the dark "counterpart of the life-womb."[225]

There are many versions of the Terrible Mother. She is the one who doesn't nurture but poisons—often the very food one would have liked to be fed. Instead of love and care she threatens to swallow or spoil, persecute or kill. So, in a way, she presents us with the dark side of the unconscious, the danger of going crazy and of death. The Terrible Mother is a representation of the unconscious in its most frightening aspect. Sometimes we need to run away from her to develop our conscious ego, rather than dwelling in the harmonious sleep of unconsciousness.

Some of the most prominent negative mother complexes I have encountered have been among the sons and daughters of mothers who suffered but survived the Nazi atrocities. Many Holocaust victims were determined to create life, finding the motif of rebirth in the creation of the

---

[224] Neumann, *The Great Mother,* p. 153.
[225] Ibid., p. 166.

modern state of Israel after the annihilation of Jewish life in Europe.

For many, however, the phoenix never arose from the ashes of the great fire *(holocaust* means, literally, that fire has destroyed everything), not even in the country that bears its name, Phoenicia.[226] They never really returned to life from "the planet called Auschwitz" (as the Israeli author and survivor Ka-Tzetnik has termed it).[227] Post-Auschwitz became a spiritless and inconsolable wandering along a wretched road over which Doomsday had already passed.

Deborah was nineteen when released from the death camp, physically in comparatively good condition and with some strength, but broken in spirit, the lone survivor of her immediate family. She was found in a displaced persons camp by a distant relative who brought her to Israel, where she worked with an older, childless widower whom she later married.

She was determined not to bring children into this horrifying world, in spite of her husband's desire, and had several miscarriages. Eventually, at the age of thirty-eight, having lived half her life after liberation, she gave birth to a son, Avner, who she proceeded to prepare for life in a world of fear, threat and death. Her preparations did not serve him well. She was convinced, or so it seemed to Avner, who was thirty-three when he came for therapy, that survival could only be assured if one was "well-behaved, blond and blue-eyed." Since he was neither blond nor blue-eyed, he always felt his existence was threatened and that he was never good enough. He would inevitably fail. What remained was to behave extremely well and repress all expressions of aggression (which is particularly noticeable in a pushy society like Israel).

Avner's identity became split. He knew he could survive only temporarily by behaving in a way that would satisfy and calm his mother. In the long run, something would destroy him, since he did not have an "Aryan look." His split-off aggression became a dark shadow, appearing as a personification of a Nazi, who would cruelly and derogatorily criticize him, often during the day, constantly at night, about practically everything.

---

[226] Phoenicia stretches along the eastern coast of the Mediterranean, through Lebanon south to the northern part of Israel.

[227] See, for instance, Ka-Tzetnik, *Shivitti*, p. x. Ka-Tzetnick was the pen-name of Yechiel Dinur, taken from the German language abbreviation for concentration camp *(Kongentrezionslager,* KZ). When testifying at the Eichmann trial, he spoke of "planet Auschwitz" to describe the camp.

When reading him stories, his mother's mind would often wander, the stories ending in Auschwitz. Avner remembers vividly the slow, dreamlike tones of his mother.

> Not everything was frightening, though most was. The stories only served as a prelude—I always knew where it would take her, but not what the story would be like. It could be any kind of everyday event, nothing special, or the smell, or the terrible dogs, or the fear of looking someone in the eyes.

He recalled a fantasy he used to have in early adolescence, in which he becomes "smaller and smaller, until I become a baby in my mother's arms. She sits on a cold metal chair in a dark, cold and damp basement. She becomes one with the metal chair, her arms cold and metallic." The world was full of dangers, and there was no protection. His father was too old and weak to make up for his mother's fears and haunting memories.

Avner was a highly qualified professional doing laboratory research. He had a strong need to stand on firm, empirical ground, which his research work provided him with. However, he had never had a fulfilling experience with a woman. He looked at women with dismay, fearing they would in some way deceive him. They could not be trusted. It seemed to Avner that they would always lead him to places where he could not preserve a sense of identity.

During six months of therapy there was an endless outpour of horror and nightmares. I was greatly concerned, feeling that his mother complex, with its core in his mother's indescribable trauma, threatened to invade his ego. The following is one recurrent dream,

> I am working on paving a new road. It's heavy and tiring. We have to make a turn, and behind a hill I see what looks like a peasant woman. She seems nice. As we come closer, I see it's my mother. When I look at her, her face and body change and she becomes the skeleton walking out of Auschwitz.

Here is another characteristic dream:

> I enter into a huge park. As I get to the far end, a gate closes behind me, and I see a sign that says "Hell." I see wormlike rats creeping over the body of a dying animal, can't see what kind. There is a strange dog, weak and starved, with the face of my mother. I don't know if it also is dying, probably, and I don't know if I should kill it or save it.

Avner carried his mother's trauma as his complex. He carried her depression and fear of life.

After half a year, Avner abruptly told me he wanted to stop analysis. I agreed, trying to ensure he felt secure enough to turn to me, or someone else, when able to do so or if in need. I did not hear from him again until almost a year later, when he called to make a "one-time" appointment. He came to tell me that he had started reading, compulsively, about the Nazi era, and particularly witnesses' accounts from Auschwitz-Birkenau. He had then tried to speak to his mother, who initially was reluctant, "as if she had forgotten that she tried to tell me everything when I was a child." She eventually opened up, and Avner said he had come to a better understanding of her, yet was still angry that she had "forced me to Auschwitz when I was a child." I was pleased that he could express at least a tiny bit of anger. He then told me that he had recently met a woman with a similar background, who seemed to resemble him in character.

I felt an urge to suggest he remain in therapy, but refrained from doing so, aware that my countertransferential wish must yield to his transferential need to stand up for himself and walk away freely.

Franz Kafka's *Letter to Father*

It would be hard to conceive of a more vivid description of a negative father complex than Kafka's *Letter to Father*. One study refers to it as showing "an uncanny level of self-revelation."[228] Kafka had actually intended to have his mother hand it over to his father, hoping to clear up their relationship. But his friend Max Brod notes:

> In reality the opposite would probably have happened. The explanation of himself to his father that the letter aimed at would never have been achieved. And Franz's mother did not pass on the letter but gave it back to him, probably with a few comforting words.[229]

Kafka primarily identified with his maternal ancestors, the Löwys, whom he saw as representing sensitivity and intelligence. However, he also found in himself

> a certain Kafka foundation [shrewd and aggressive in business] that, however, just isn't set in motion by the Kafka *will to life*, *business* and *conquest*, but by a Löwy spur that operates more secretively, more timidly, and in a different direction, and which often fails to work at all.[230]

---

[228] Mairowitz and Crumb, *Introducing Kafka*, p. 159.
[229] *Franz Kafka: A Biography*, p. 16.
[230] *Letter to Father*, p. 12 (italics added).

That is, his father identification was not activated, due to his lack of extraverted (business) and aggressive (conquest) energy (will to life). While Kafka was extremely sensitive and introverted, his father was extraverted, depicted by Franz as

> a true Kafka in strength, health, appetite, loudness of voice, eloquence, self-satisfaction, worldly superiority, stamina, presence of mind, knowledge of human nature, a certain generosity.[231]

Lest we be tempted to believe Franz idealized his father, he quickly corrects this impression, adding that father also possesses "all the failings and weaknesses that go with these advantages, into which your temperament and sometimes your violent temper drive you."[232]

Max Brod and others have criticized Kafka's description of his father for being exaggerated. Brod says,

> Here and there I feel the perspective is distorted, unsupported assumptions are occasionally dragged in and made to fit the facts; on what appear to be negligible, immediate reactions, a whole edifice is built up, the ramifications of which it is impossible to grasp as a whole, which in fact in the end definitely turns on its own axis and contradicts itself, and yet manages to stand erect on its own foundation.[233]

Of course Kafka's description is exaggerated, self-contradictory and yet "stands erect on its own foundation!" This merely reflects that we are dealing not with a scientific description of the object, as if there were such a thing, but with Kafka's *imago* of his father, and seemingly unbeknownst to himself Brod here draws the very contours of an autonomous complex.

Kafka's father is perceived through the tinted lens of his complex. As complex and object interact in the psyche, perceptions will be drawn into the complex and cluster around its core. This does not necessarily mean that Kafka's view of his father is entirely wrong or distorted. Portraying his father, Kafka himself says, "I am speaking only of the image through which you influenced the child."[234]

As is evident from the portrait he draws, it is a small child's view of a big invincible Father. Kafka's conscious sense of identity collapses under

---

[231] Ibid.
[232] Ibid.
[233] *Franz Kafka: A Biography*, p. 17.
[234] *Letter to Father*, p. 13.

the weight of the powerful complex. His father was, writes Kafka,

> too strong for me, especially since my brothers died young, my sisters only
> arrived much later, so that I had to endure the first knock or two all alone,
> and for that I was much too weak.[235]

Franz does not put the entire blame on his father for whom he, Franz,
had become, because, he says, "even if I had grown up entirely free of
your influence . . . I would probably still have become a weakly, timid,
hesitant, restless person."[236]

However, were it not for feeling tyrannized by a domineering father of
opposite psychological type, he might have gained a different attitude and
a better sense of self-acceptance. All his life the introverted Kafka strug-
gled to gain a foothold in the extraverted world of his father, for instance
in his job with the Workers Accident Insurance Institute.

Although the family was financially well off, it was taken for granted
that Kafka would not "be a burden on his parents' pockets a day longer
than was necessary."[237] Paradoxically the very introversion of his energy,
by means of which Kafka searched his soul and brought forth the classic
images of suffering and alienation that have come to represent the modern
era, prevented him from dedicating himself altogether to writing. Brod
terms this inability to stand up for his true self "the fatal weakness of his
life."[238] Anthony Storr[239] compares Kafka's statement, "There's never
been a time in which I have been convinced from within myself that I am
alive," with Jung's: "Personality is the supreme realization of the innate
idiosyncrasy of a living being."[240]

The father, Hermann Kafka, seems to have had a firm foothold in the
outer world. His son Franz did not. His personality was predominantly
schizoid. Introverted, with highly developed intuition (and thinking as
auxiliary function), he was the very opposite of his father. As Daryl Sharp
notes, an introverted intuitive, with a therefore extraverted sensation as his
inferior function, is "bound to have difficulty accepting his existential re-

---

[235] Ibid., p. 11.
[236] Ibid.
[237] Brod, *Franz Kafka: A Biography,* p. 78.
[238] Ibid.
[239] *Churchill's Black Dog,* p. 53.
[240] "The Development of Personality," *The Development of Personality,* CW 17,
par. 289.

ality."[241] His father's lack of understanding of the differences between them made the burden even heavier.

When a child is of a discernibly different psychological type than the rest of the family, this may provide fertile ground for the growth of an autonomous complex. If the child's dominant attitude (introversion or extraversion) and function (thinking, feeling, sensation or intuition) deviate from those of the others, and if this difference is negatively received, the development of a stable, separate identity may be impaired.[242] The introverted boy, who prefers reading to sports or camping, might be seen as weird by other family members with a dominant interest in hiking and outdoor activities (extraverted sensation). Similarly, an active, extraverted girl who loves sports, growing up in a family that mainly values classical music and literature, might be no better off.

Kafka was unable to uphold his own separate identity vis-à-vis his domineering father. It is amazing how in that relationship the otherwise so perceptive Kafka suffered from a lowering of awareness, an *abaissement de niveau mental*. Kafka says, in the beginning of his letter, "You once asked me recently why I claim to be afraid of you. I did not know, as usual, what to answer, partly out of my fear of you."[243] And later he writes, "I acquired in your presence . . . a hesitant, stammering manner of speaking, and even that was too much for you . . . I could neither think nor speak in your presence."[244]

Kafka was afraid and the fear paralyzed him. The terrifying complex—Brod speaks of an "infantile complex"[245]—directly attacks consciousness and detracts available energy from the ego. When in the grip of the complex, ego-consciousness and identity are impaired. Feeling is then no longer a value-judgment, and affect and sensitivity overtake us. We are overcome by fear, rage or the like, and tend to project.

Kafka feels his father "exposes" him by "indiscriminately" speaking about his son in front of others. Hermann sees himself as the hardworking father who sacrifices all to his ungrateful son. The feeling of being exposed is common when a complex is activated, and conversely, complexes

---

[241] *The Secret Raven: Conflict and Transformation in Franz Kafka.*, p. 78.
[242] See Storr, *Churchill's Black Dog,* pp. 52ff.
[243] *Letter to Father,* p. 7.
[244] Ibid., p. 22.
[245] *Franz Kafka: A Biography,* p. 24.

are activated by exposure. The child's exposure to archaic fears is often seen in sleep disturbances. Gerhard Adler, for instance, writes:

> Nearly all children practice certain peculiar ceremonies, especially at bedtime, for the transition from waking to sleeping is of particular importance, representing as it does the mysterious moment of transition from light to darkness. . . . These puerilities . . . are, properly considered, survivals of magic apotropaic, that is protective ceremonies, customary in primitive races. Just because a child has an instinctive knowledge of the minuteness of its own small ego as opposed to the primeval force of the collective powers, it seeks by means of such ceremonies before going to sleep to ensure that its tiny ego will not be completely reabsorbed into the lap of the great primeval night.[246]

Oedipus, and so many other heroes, are exposed to "the lap of the great primeval night," from which they are barely saved. We do not hear of those who do not survive. We meet others, severely wounded, in the psychiatric ward. Especially for a shy and sensitive child, such as Franz Kafka, the blunt exposure to ridicule and reprimand of the adult world of his father's friends implies being eradicated, torn up by the roots. This is the defenseless child who is not related to with consideration, exposed by having his vulnerable persona ripped off. The feeling of exposure means a loss of defenses, and is a main feature in trauma. It prevents the constructive task of the complexes, and coalesces into a constantly open wound.

Later Kafka describes his father as

> that enormous man, . . . the ultimate authority, [who] could for almost no reason come during the night and take me out of bed and carry me out onto the pavlatche [a courtyard gallery connecting several apartments], and that meant I was a mere nothing to him.[247]

This is the kind of fear the overwhelming, ego-shattering complex evokes: to be taken away by the "enormous man" and the "ultimate authority," with no ego to stand up against those greater forces. It is reflected in not knowing what to answer or in the feeling of being "a mere nothing" (though Kafka does observe that the feeling of nothingness may in some respects be "noble and fruitful").

The proportions seem exaggerated from a purely empirical perspective,

---

[246] *Studies in Analytical Psychology*, pp. 122f.
[247] *Letter to Father*, p. 14.

"and I lean toward this exaggeration," says Kafka, but from the perspective of the complex-ridden ego, the "I" becomes dwarf-like and minute in comparison to the giant, beast-like and monstrous complex-evoking object. Comparing himself with his father, as Kafka does over and over again, he is the "slowly developing child," while his father is "the completed man," whom one "could have presumed . . . would simply trample me into the ground until nothing remained of me."[248]

To Kafka it is clear that his father would want his son to be of a different breed than the weak, sensitive and fearful person he was. "You wanted me to be a strong, brave boy,"[249] he says, in painful recognition of his inability to live up to such expectations. "You encouraged me . . . when I saluted and marched smartly, but I was no future soldier,"[250] he says, helplessly resigned. The negativity of Kafka's father complex does not emanate only from the two of them being of different constitution and psychological type, but also from the father's *attitude,* in effect demanding that the son renounce his own identity.

One's capacity to assimilate into consciousness the complex material that arises from the Self depends on the ego's relative freedom. In Kafka's case, his ego lacked the necessary "will of life" to assertively stand up for himself.[251] The ego did not provide the firm ground his true self would have needed in order to bear exposure to daylight. Storr puts it thus,

> Overadaptation to the other means loss of the self as a separate entity. Only in the silent watches of the night, when Kafka was entirely alone, could he get in touch with his innermost depths and be really and truly himself.[252]

Tainted by his oppressive father complex, Kafka was ambivalent toward his inner world, shedding light on it only in darkness. He was equally ambivalent toward his father's extraversion, as when he says:

> I would have needed a little encouragement, a little friendliness, a little keeping open of my path; instead you obstructed it for me, with the good intention, it is true, of making me take a different path.[253]

---

[248] Ibid., p. 13.
[249] Ibid.
[250] Ibid., p. 15.
[251] Ibid., p. 12.
[252] *Churchill's Black Dog,* p. 72.
[253] *Letter to Father,* p. 15.

His whole letter, that remained unsent because his mother felt it would not be received the way Kafka needed, is an appeal to be accepted by Father.

Kafka was not able to write in daytime, apart from the fact that descending into the depths of soul is a dark-time and night-place activity. Nor was he really able to publish his books,[254] requesting that they be incinerated after his death. Max Brod, however, disobeyed his friend's will, and we might wonder, if Kafka really wanted them set on fire, why he didn't he strike the match himself. He had posed the same request to Dora Diamant, the only woman who managed to take Kafka away, at last, from his parental home. Ironically, the Gestapo carried out his wish, confiscating manuscripts of his in a raid on Diamant's Berlin apartment in 1933.[255]

Kafka describes a childhood incident when he "kept on whimpering for water." When threats did not made him stop, he was left standing alone in his nightshirt outside the locked door. We can imagine the fear and the terror overtaking the child, as he stands there punished, locked out in the night. It easily reminds us of Kafka's anti-hero Josef K., who will forever wait outside the door, never to be admitted, not knowing his crime. "After that," writes Kafka in regard to his childhood memory, "I was really quite obedient, but I came away from it with internal damage."[256] Kafka learned to split off shadow parts of himself, becoming, instead, "quite obedient." That is, his ego was drawn into the domain of his internalized father. Rather than being constructively nourished by the complexes journeying from archetypal lands, unfolding into his conscious identity, the latter was in the grip of the powerful father complex. He consciously sided with an ego-ideal set by his father's standards, to the detriment of self-acceptance.

Like the ego, the complexes have their seat in the body and the body image. Thus, the power of the complex over the ego is expressed physically. Kafka writes:

> I was . . . already weighed down by your sheer physical presence. I remember, for example, how we often undressed together in the same changing-room. I was skinny, weakly, slight; you were strong, tall, broad. . . . I holding your hand, a small skeleton, insecure, barefoot on the planks, afraid of the water."[257]

---

[254] In Hebrew, to publish a book is to "bring into light."
[255] Mairowitz and Crumb, *Introducing Kafka*, p. 155.
[256] *Letter to Father*, p. 14.
[257] Ibid., pp. 15f.

From his complex-ridden body image we cannot easily imagine the tall and handsome man he was. As Storr says, "His feeling of physical inferiority dated from childhood, and was emotionally determined, not based upon reality."[258]

The affect of the complex often pertains to instinctual aspects, feelings of disgust and aversion. For instance, Kafka vividly describes his father's presence at the dinner table:

> You, in accordance with your strong appetite . . . ate everything quickly, hot and in big mouthfuls. . . . We were not allowed to slurp vinegar, you were. The main thing was that the bread be cut straight; but that you did it with a knife dripping with gravy was immaterial. . . . At the table we were only allowed to eat, but you cleaned and clipped your fingernails, . . . cleaned your ears with a toothpick.[259]

There is a double standard, the imposition of a yardstick that has nothing to do with relatedness, but rather with the tyranny of an oppressive persona and collective consciousness: "Your lessons were for the most part lessons on correct table manners."[260] There is a wavering back and forth, between whether to revolt against his father's standards, or to submit: "You were for me the standard by which everything was measured";[261] "You, the authority on everything";[262] "Everything that you shouted at me was virtually a commandment from heaven."[263]

Kafka located his father's yardstick within the confines of his negative father complex and internalized father-*imago*. "You took on that enigmatic something," he writes, "that all tyrants have whose law is founded on their person, not their reasoning."[264] And more:

> The world came to be divided into three parts for me, one in which I, the slave, lived under laws that had been invented only for me and moreover which I could, I didn't know why, never fully comply with, then a second world, infinitely distant from mine, in which you lived, preoccupied with government, with the issuing of orders and with the annoyance at their not

---

[258] *Churchill's Black Dog,* pp. 57f.
[259] *Letter to Father,* pp. 19f.
[260] Ibid., p. 19.
[261] Ibid., p. 16.
[262] Ibid., p. 18.
[263] Ibid., p. 19.
[264] Ibid., p. 17.

being obeyed, and finally a third world wherein everyone else lived happily and free from orders and from having to obey.[265]

"The father," says Jung, "represents the world of moral commandments and prohibitions":

> [He] is the representative of the spirit, whose function it is to oppose pure instinctuality. That is his archetypal role, which falls to him regardless of his personal qualities; hence he is very often an object of neurotic fears for the son. Accordingly, the monster to be overcome by the son frequently appears as a giant who guards the treasure.[266]

In Kafka's case, since his father did seem to personify an overweight of the negative father, the spiritual father principle has been split. Therefore, at the center of Kafka's complex we find the archetypal image of the cruel king or tyrant. Kafka's father could not serve as guide, as pathfinder into the ways of the world. He was not able to help his introverted son cope more successfully in outer life without ridding him of his true identity. His father did not *see* Kafka, in the sense of enabling him to be sufficiently related to his own true nature. Indeed, Kafka's father himself appears to be a prime example of the inauthenticity that goes hand in hand with persona identification and collective consciousness.

In fact, as Thomas Anz notes in his afterword to Kafka's *Letter* (referring among others to the psychoanalyst Paul Federn's 1919 essay, "On the Psychology of the Revolution: The Fatherless Society"),[267] the era was one of challenging the father and collective consciousness. This was strongly felt in Jewish communities, where the heavily father-based society went through a major upheaval at the turn of the last century. The flame of Zionism that burned in many Jewish communities (along with the idea of America as the "Golden Country," or Kafka's fantasy expressed in his novel *Amerika),* most distinctly signified the breakaway from paternal law and authority, challenging the father's spiritual rule as well as his dominion over earthly matters.

Zionism aimed at implementing a nonmaterialistic society based on the return to a spiritualized Mother Earth in the ancient homeland.[268] Kafka

---

[265] Ibid., p. 20.

[266] *Symbols of Transformation,* CW 5, par. 396.

[267] *Letter to Father,* p. 85.

[268] See Shalit, *The Hero and His Shadow,* pp. 36ff

actually toyed with the idea of emigrating to Palestine and opening a restaurant in Tel Aviv, where Dora would cook and Kafka himself be the waiter. However, that remained yet another unrealized fantasy, which his less charismatic but more pragmatic friend Max Brod came to carry out, at least in part, for instance as advisor to Habima, the national theater.

The mere idea of marriage and family, "the highest one can achieve," remained an unfulfilled dream, another unresolved aspect of Kafka's father complex, because,

> I'd be your equal, every old and eternally new shame and tyranny would be mere history. It would indeed be like a fairy tale, but precisely therein lies the questionable element.[269]

His difficulty with women, whom he saw as "snares which lie in wait for men on all sides,"[270] is of course primarily related to Kafka's mother complex, which has been analyzed in detail by Daryl Sharp.

Kafka relates the lack of spiritual guidance to his father's attitude toward religion. "What kind of Judaism was it that I got from you!" He accuses his father of hypocrisy, "a mere trifle, a joke, not even a joke," indifference, and turning worship into business meetings.[271] There is a certain tone of understanding, though, seeing "those few trivialities you performed in the name of Judaism . . . as small souvenirs of earlier times."[272] Kafka makes a sociological observation as well, when he relates his father's conduct to a transitional generation of Jews that migrated from the villages into the cities, and in many cases to the New World.

However, when Kafka later searched for a deeper sense of meaning in Judaism he was met with "negative high esteem for my new Judaism."[273] Kafka would have wanted the religion of the Fathers to serve as a connecting link between him and his own father. He thought that in Judaism,

> deliverance would have been conceivable, in principle, but what is more, it would have been conceivable for us to find one another in Judaism or we might even have started out from there in harmony.[274]

---

[269] *Letter to Father*, p. 64.
[270] Journal entry quoted in Sharp, *The Secret Raven*, p. 37.
[271] *Letter to Father*, p. 44.
[272] Ibid., p. 49
[273] Ibid., p. 51.
[274] Ibid., p. 44.

He of course came to feel disappointed and rejected by his father. "Because of my connection with it, Judaism became repulsive to you, Jewish writings unreadable, they 'nauseated' you."[275] But he is aware, as well, that were his father to show an interest, he himself would turn away. The father complex would take precedence and destroy the deeper meaning, the relationship to the Self.

While the constructive complex serves as link between Self and ego, as the path for the archetype to enter the realm of the personal, the autonomous complex becomes disruptive. It becomes an obstacle in the ego-Self relationship, thereby hampering the individuation process. The negative father-*imago* becomes an oppressive agent of collective consciousness, of the norms and rules to be obeyed, and of falseness. Along the two axes of father that Samuels describes,[276] strong-weak and castrating-facilitating, Kafka's father is clearly strong and castrating.

The autonomous complex has a tendency to gather strength and spread out, to pertain to all and every strand of life, even if seemingly unrelated. In Kafka's complex, the father is the measurement and the yardstick, both governor and judge, all-encompassing. Kafka imagined his father's body spread out across a map of the world. Father comes to personify the outer, social world. It is the shadow of condemnation, tyranny, invincibility and alienation in the father-*imago* and in the father-society that Kafka has depicted so penetratingly and surrealistically in his writings.

Kafka never really succeeded in breaking away from home, which is necessary in order to separate from the parental complexes. As noted, along with his negative father complex, Kafka was also captive to his mother complex, which "cut him off from life."[277] He had no opportunity, he says, to distinguish himself as his father had, which can be done only through "violence and subversion" and by "break[ing] away from home,"[278] neither of which he was capable of. External success meant much less to Kafka than his father's (non-existent) approval, and did not create any sense of self-confidence. Reality and actual experience do not alter a powerful autonomous complex. Rather, the complex distorts the perception of reality and the ensuing interaction between self and object.

---

[275] Ibid., pp. 50f.
[276] *The Father*, pp. 23f.
[277] Sharp, *The Secret Raven*, p. 82.
[278] *Letter to Father*, p. 32.

I was always convinced—and I had positive proof of it in your cold expression—that the more I succeeded, the worse it would have to turn out. Often in my mind's eye I saw the terrible assembly of the teachers as they would meet when I'd passed the first class, and then in the second class, when I'd passed that, and then in the third and so on, in order to examine this unique, outrageous case, how I, the most incapable and, in any case, the most ignorant of all, had succeeded in creeping up so far as this class, which, now that everyone's attention was fixed on me, would of course instantly spew me out, to the jubilation of all the righteous, now liberated from this nightmare. To live with such fantasies is not easy for a child.[279]

Nor, we might add, for an adult either, when burdened by such a powerful complex. However, while *Letter To Father* gives us remarkable insight into the world of complexes, we must bear in mind that it is through the prism of his complex that Kafka portrayed the despiritualized father archetype. John Updike quotes Gustav Janouch asking Kafka if his work might be "a mirror of tomorrow," upon which Kafka "covered his eyes with his hands and rocked back and forth, saying, 'You are right. . . . Probably that's why I can't finish anything. I am afraid of the truth.' "[280]

And later, Updike quotes Janouch listening to Kafka as they pass the Old Synagogue in Prague (which Hitler intended to turn into a "museum of a vanished race"), and hearing Kafka announce that men "will try to grind the synagogue to dust by destroying the Jews themselves."[281]

By means of his creativity, introverted intuition, unintegrated complex and scrupulous self-examination, Kafka gave expression to the shadow-side of the father archetype, the oppression, alienation and belittlement, that has put its mark on modern man.

Inflation, Hubris and the Tower of Babel

Inflation

We speak of inflation when a person's conscious sense of identity, one's "I," has taken upon itself too many unconscious contents. Jung:

An inflated consciousness is always egocentric and conscious of nothing but its own existence. . . . It is hypnotized by itself and therefore cannot be argued with. It inevitably dooms itself to calamities that must strike it dead.

---

[279] Ibid., p. 54f.
[280] Foreword in Nahum Glatzer, ed., *Franz Kafka: The Complete Stories,* p. xix.
[281] Ibid.

Paradoxically enough, inflation is a regression of consciousness into unconsciousness.[282]

The inflated ego is undifferentiated. It does not discriminate between ego and Self, nor does it distinguish between polarities, such as good and evil. It assumes godlike proportions, approving of the Commandment to have "no other gods before me," where "me" means the ego.

An essential component of ego-formation is the establishment of boundaries. When inflated, however, the ego does not realize its limitations. In fact, it is possessed by compensatory unconscious forces. While the conscious ego seems narcissistic and grandiose, underneath the surface linger compensatory, gnawing doubts and feelings of inferiority. Thus unrecognized autonomous complexes take their revenge. (In so-called negative inflation, one suffers from an "unrealistically low opinion of oneself,"[283] due to identification with negative shadow contents.)

Hubris

The ancient Greeks called inflation *hybris*. They considered arrogance, pride and defiance of the gods the one great sin. Edinger defines it thus:

It is the human arrogance that appropriates to man what belongs to the gods, or in psychological terms appropriates to the ego what belongs to the transpersonal level of the psyche.[284]

However, as he goes on to say,

Just the presumption for an ego to come into existence at all and to claim itself as a separate center of conscious being is replete with *hybris*, and this psychological fact links with the imagery of original sin.[285]

Perhaps hubris is still our greatest sin. Since we have at our disposal tools of unprecedented power, hubris poses greater global danger than ever. Scientific humanity can defy the forces of nature, interfering without restrain, claiming godly rights.[286] Jung was acutely concerned with man's potential for ill, as he expressed in his "Face to Face" interview:

---

[282] *Psychology and Alchemy,* CW 12, par. 563.
[283] Daryl Sharp, *Jung Lexicon:A Primer of Terms and Concepts,* p. 87.
[284] *The Eternal Drama,* p. 96.
[285] Ibid.
[286] See Shalit, *Shadows in Jerusalem: Beyond the Hill of Evil Counsel, Towards the Valley of Hell.*

The only real danger that exists is man himself. He is the great danger, and
we are pitifully unaware of it. . . . His psyche should be studied, because we
are the origin of all coming evil.[287]

And he was keenly aware of the catastrophic hazards that hubris entails. Late in life, he writes,

At the end of the second millennium the outlines of a universal catastrophe
became apparent, at first in the form of a threat to consciousness. This threat
consists in giantism—in other words, a hubris of consciousness—in the assertion: "Nothing is greater than man and his deeds."[288]

It seems urgent for us to realize, that the transcendent "nothing" is, in
fact, greater than us and our deeds.

Nemesis, daughter of the Night (thus sister to Hypnos and Thanatos, as
well as to Eros; that is, sleep, death and love), goddess of retribution, provided the vengeance of the gods. That is, she represents the archetypal
principle by which the objective psyche takes revenge when humanity
becomes inflated. Her compensatory treatment for hubris is often a harsh
downfall. It is unquestionably more healthy if we can implement appropriate ego-boundaries from within.

Ego-boundaries are, essentially, body-boundaries. They constitute limi-
tation in space. They are also boundaries of consciousness. Furthermore,
they are boundaries of humbleness, honoring the necessary relationship
with the elements and the transcendent, acknowledging the shadow as well
as morality, mortality and imperfection. A person or a society that consciously acknowledges the ego's limitations fares far better than when
Nemesis forces herself upon one from without. When for instance the
world soul is wounded and hits back invasively, because her breath of air
and oceanic embrace have been polluted and the wings of her soul broken,
trembling under the yoke of the shadow that we have carelessly and arro-
gantly dumped on her, then the punishment might be much harsher than
we can survive.

The Tower of Babel

The Biblical image of hubris is the erection of the Tower of Babel. The
story is told in Genesis as follows:

---

[287] McGuire and Hull, eds., *C.G. Jung Speaking,* p. 436.
[288] *Memories, Dreams, Reflections,* p. 328.

And the whole earth was of one language, and of one speech.

And it came to pass, as they journeyed from the east, that they found a plain in the land of Shinar; and they dwelt there.

And they said one to another, Go to, let us make bricks, and burn them thoroughly. And they had brick for stone, and slime had they for mortar.

And they said, Go to, let us build us a city and a tower, whose top may reach unto heaven; and let us make us a name, lest we be scattered abroad upon the face of the whole earth.

And the Lord came down to see the city and the tower, which the children of men builded.

And the Lord said, Behold, the people are one, and they have all one language; and this they begin to do; and now nothing will be restrained from them, which they have imagined to do.

Go to, let us go down, and there confound their language, that they may not understand one another's speech.

So the Lord scattered them abroad from thence upon the face of all the earth; and they left off to build the city.

Therefore is the name of it called Babel, because the Lord did there confound the language of all the earth; and from thence did the Lord scatter them abroad upon the face of all the earth. (11:1-9; AV)

The people were allowed "to burn the bricks thoroughly," that is, to make use of the Promethean fire of consciousness. But when they became inflated, God interfered in the project and caused disarray and confusion by having them become incapable of understanding each other's language. The Tower of Babel, the Gate to Heaven, collapsed, and confusion (in Hebrew, *balbel)* ensued.

Reaching heaven may reflect our desire to *reach for* God rather than the intention to take His place, unlike the act of hubris, as told in Isaiah:

How art thou fallen from heaven, O Shahar, son of the morning! . . . For thou hast said in thine heart, I will ascend to heaven, I will exalt my throne above the stars of God: . . . I will ascend above the heights of the clouds; I will be like the most high. (14:12-15; AV)

The fall of Shahar from heaven, or in his Christian designation, Lucifer, the bringer of light, is a consequence of his hubris. The fall from hubris makes us descend into hell. The striving for "godlike heights" is "certain to be followed by an equally deep plunge into the abyss," says Jung.[289]

---

[289] *Two Essays on Analytical Psychology, CW 7, par. 41.*

Yet, as Edinger notes, "having a built-in God-image, man will strive to be godlike."[290] And the bringing of the light of consciousness entails hubris. In fact, God's very punishment, scattering man on the face of the earth and the division into different languages, "represents a process of differentiation arising out of original homogeneity,"[291] thus instigating a movement toward consciousness.

The peak of hubris was perhaps not the actual building of the tower, but the urge to "make us a name," which must be considered as challenging God, since in Judaism God is "The Name." Gershom Scholem says,

> For this is the real and, if I may say so, the peculiarly Jewish object of mystical contemplation: The Name of God, which is something absolute, because it reflects the hidden meaning and totality of existence; the Name through which everything else acquires its meaning and which yet to the human mind has no concrete, particular meaning of its own.[292]

And later he quotes the Kabbalist Abraham Abulafia (born in Saragossa, 1240), "wishing to honor the glorious Name by serving it with the life of body and soul, veil thy face and be afraid to look at God."[293]

Thus, reaching up to heaven to "make us a name" in order to retain original unity and wholeness ("lest we be scattered"), indicates the hubris of narcissistic ego-inflation.

Inflated Ego—Emptied Self

Ehud is forty years old, married with three young children. At age twenty-one, after finishing his army service, he left the kibbutz in which he grew up. After university studies he worked for some years for an advertising company, eventually setting up his own, very successful agency.

He is a high achiever, very demanding of himself and constantly desiring success. He has a strong need for narcissistic gratification, to be admired and respected. He considers himself "capable of anything," but the last several years, along with considerable financial and professional success, have brought increasing fears of failure. He has frequent anxiety attacks, fearing different kinds of breakdown. He is afraid that his façade, or persona, of coping and accomplishment will crack, and that people will

---

[290] *The Bible and the Psyche,* p. 23.
[291] Ibid.
[292] *Major Trends in Jewish Mysticism,* p. 133.
[293] Ibid., p. 137.

find out that he is a "nut-case." "To have a breakdown is bad enough, but if others find out, you're doomed," he says.

He feels threatened by an inner sense of weakness, afraid he will faint in public places, that his legs will start to shake and he will fall. He finds the possibility of losing control dreadful. He is scared his car will break down when there is no one there to help him, "and even worse if someone *would* be there to help, to see me helpless." Worst of all is his fear of having an anxiety attack, which, he says, "looks like something but is nothing." He is afraid of the emptiness and the nothingness behind his external mask of success. An anxiety attack, which people might mistakenly take for a heart-attack, would disclose his lack of inner connectedness, reveal there is "nothing there."

In one dream he stays in a fashionable house, with an outpour of gibberish through the loudspeakers. He knows that he is supposed to do something, but does not understand what. He makes believe *as if* he knows, but in the dream this makes him feel great danger. He knows the alternative is to be thrown out, where the rain pours down. His inflated, "fashionable" ego consists mainly of an outpouring of meaningless gibberish and falseness, "as-if." It would do him well to consciously step outside his ego and feel the rain.

About a year prior to therapy Ehud started developing compulsive rituals "to appease God," who might want to punish him. He wanted to figure out "God's scheme," he said, so that he could do "the right thing." For Ehud, to do the right thing meant to dwell on senseless counting and number combinations, along with other obsessive thoughts and compulsive acts, rather than a pursuit for meaning. Thus, he said, he would be able to outdo God, and hopefully gain immortality. While laughing at himself, not unaware of his hubris, he did believe that if only he could manage to stay well and healthy, science would eventually grant him immortality.

As a small child, the youngest of three, he had been shy and withdrawn. In mid-puberty his behavior changed dramatically. He became outgoing, assertive and one of the leaders of his peer group. His axiomatic motto was, "No one must know anything that can be held against you, no weakness and nothing embarrassing—it never wears off, a stigma forever."

Like many who have grown up in a collective community, Ehud complained about his lack of mothering. "My mother is so weak she can't really be blamed," he acknowledged, "but I can't understand how you can leave a little child crying at night in the children's home without looking after him." While children of the kibbutz were raised collectively, particularly in the past, there were parents, especially mothers, who found it hard to adjust to these arrangements. Others, like Ehud's mother, found it suitable and convenient not to have to carry the sole burden of motherhood. This enabled many, including Ehud's mother who was nurse-in-charge at the kibbutz clinic, to devote themselves fully to their professional activities, ensuring "the emancipation of the woman from the yoke of domestic service."[294] As Bruno Bettelheim notes, it may well have relieved much of the anxiety that naturally comes with motherhood. He explores the ambivalence kibbutz mothers felt:

> The kibbutz woman rejected what, in the eyes of the world, was good mothering, the kind she got from her own mother. And just as any child who rejects his parents expects to be punished for it, and fears it most in regard to what was the essence of the rejection, so she may have feared she would be punished for rejecting a mother she found wanting, by turning out to be an even worse mother herself.[295]

Collective parenting in Israel belonged to a certain ideological phase. It has since largely been relinquished. Nowadays, for instance, children in the kibbutz remain with their parents until their teens, no longer sleeping in the separate "children's home." When Ehud grew up, the children's home was situated at the far end of the kibbutz, only meters away from the then unruly Jordanian border. He recalls his own and other children's feeling of "exposure," and is today unable to come to terms with what he considers to be his parents' negligence. Prior to Israel's independence, and during the early decades of statehood, Israeli children, and perhaps particularly so in the kibbutz, carried their parents' fantasy of invincibility. Therefore, what today comes across as neglect was at the time an inflated projection onto "the children of the future."

Ehud's father is a prominent leader in the large kibbutz he lives on. Ehud ridicules as anachronistic the socialist kibbutz ideology that his father pledged allegiance to, mocking the creed "from each one according to his capacity, to everyone according to their needs." Yet, he views his father as a man of incomparably high moral stature, "my own opposite." The

---

[294] Melford E. Spiro, *Children of the Kibbutz,* p. 17.
[295] *The Children of the Dream,* p. 39.

father is concerned with the welfare of the kibbutz members, helping out whenever he can, equally as devoted to tilling the fields as editing a cultural magazine, thus combining manual and intellectual work, precisely along the original kibbutz idea of "synthetic man."

Ehud claims that his father relates to others because of ideology and his moral stance, rather than sincere relatedness. He is angry at his father's commitment to the needs of the collective rather than to those of his own children. Devotion and commitment to the goals and aspirations of the collective, often at the expense of one's own children, was common among Israel's founding fathers during the formative years of Israeli society.[296] In the kibbutz, the authority of the father was altered on ideological grounds. As Melford Spiro says,

> Instead of an authoritarian-submissive father-child relationship, the kibbutz aimed to establish an egalitarian relationship in which fathers and children were to be peers.[297]

However, Ehud, as well as others who have grown up in the framework of a kibbutz, have expressed ambivalence toward this more egalitarian father-child relationship, feeling that it may entail an avoidance of paternal responsibility. (Both Spiro and Bettelheim have discussed the Oedipal effects of the non-authoritarian father in the kibbutz.) For Ehud, father is a positive persona, or a "white shadow." While of high moral stature, in contrast to his own sense of moral indifference and egotism, Ehud claims his father lacks true Eros. He also has a deep feeling that his father's way is unattainable, with no possibility of challenging him while on "father's territory."

There can hardly be a sincere Oedipal rivalry when the father solemnly personifies the norms and convictions of collective consciousness, yet does not insist on his own, personal beliefs. The symbolic death of the father may then take place through departure rather than Oedipal patricide. An unusually high proportion of those who grew up on kibbutzim have, in fact, emigrated, thus departing altogether from the realm of the personal father as well as from the Land of the Fathers.

In the kibbutz (from *kvutza,* Hebrew for "group"), the group is strongly emphasized and plays a dominant role. Especially in the past, when child-

---

[296] See Shalit, *The Hero and His Shadow,* pp. 44f.
[297] *Children of the Kibbutz,* p. 12.

rearing practices relied more on the collective than the personal parents, the group was a significant mirror.

D.W. Winnicott says,

> In individual emotional development *the precursor of the mirror is the mother's face.* . . . What does the baby see when he or she looks at the mother's face? [And he answers:] I am suggesting that, ordinarily, what the baby sees is himself or herself. In other words the mother is looking at the baby and *what she looks like is related to what she sees there.*[298]

That is, what the person who carries the mother archetype comes to look like depends on what he or she sees in the baby, which may be anything from angel to monster. Thus, what mother sees in her baby may be the self of the infant, or it may for instance be the horrors of her projected shadow or the expectations of her persona. That is, the infant may be called upon to mirror the parent rather than being the mirrored one.

We might assume that if the archetype of mother has adequately constellated, she can serve as self-object, mirroring the baby's sense of self and its sense of divinity.

Nurturing in the kibbutz nowadays is not entirely in the hands of the personal mother, though there has been a significant trend back to the family unit. Mothering and early mirroring provided by the nurses is still deeply influenced by ideology, that is, by prevailing collective values. As well, the child belongs from an early age to the so-called children's society, growing up close together with one's peer group. Therefore, the children's group constitutes an important mirror for the development of the person's conscious identity and the transmission of collective ideals.

As experienced by Ehud and others, mirroring was from an early age determined by the ego-ideal of the collective—the kibbutz at large—as transmitted through the nurses, the parents and other adults, and the peer-group. And the kibbutz ideal was a very distinct one: the self-assertive and, as if complex-free, straightforward and reticent "Sabra-personality" (named after the sabra fruit, tough and thorny on the outside, soft on the inside). If pioneering was an early ideal, later it came to include combat service, preferably in commando units or the air force (for example, while the kibbutz makes up just 2-3% of Israel's population, sometimes 15% of the graduates in pilot training are from the kibbutzim). With a distinct ego-

---

[298] *Playing and Reality,* pp. 130f.

ideal, the group comes to serve as a mirror for the persona.

In Ehud's case this caused an absence of unconditional self-acceptance. Though in no way lacking in ego-strength, this persona-mirroring failed to produce an integrated sense of ego, well-rooted and based on an inner sense of self-support. Rather, it brought about an incessant and anxious need to present a persona, even if false, to the world and to himself, of being the perfect fulfillment of the ego-ideal, thus obtaining the approval and narcissistic gratification of the admiring collective.

For Ehud, the kibbutz, its children as well as adults, members known to him as well as those unknown—that is, without differentiation—served and still serve as reference point for his ego, or rather his persona. His ego still needs to be mirrored and gain the approval of the group, which now is an entirely internalized object, or rather *imago*, since Ehud has lived all his adult life away from the kibbutz. Since his ego is disconnected from the Self, he is left with the wrappings of his persona, a false self of achievement and accomplishment, while his soul remains empty. Such an ego needs constant affirmation, since it carries the weight of the Self. In its hubristic state, the narcissistically inflated ego is constantly threatened with a fall off the wall, like Humpty-Dumpty.

For several years Ehud had been able to keep his mounting anxiety at bay by simply doing "more of the same," that is, expanding his already inflated, persona-possessed ego complex. His advertising agency, dealing as it does with appearance and persona, just *had to* grow, and every evening he calculated its size by his employees' daily working hours. He bought a bigger house, fancier cars, attended more parties with "who's who." For some time anxiety woke him occasionally at night, but was soon brushed off by his ego-in-hubris in the light of day. Repetitive dreams of climbing a steep mountain, scared to death as he is thrown back near the top by rolling stones or caught in an avalanche, did not lead him to ponder the meaningless labor of Sisyphus.

It was then that he turned to obsessive counting rituals, to appease the punitive God-image that tormented him. As Jung says, symptoms are the soul's effort at healing. But even this did not make him aware of the extent to which his ego would go to ward off the Self.

Eventually Ehud became completely unable to be alone, neither at home nor at work, not while driving or when going for a walk. When alone, anxiety would flood in and overtake him; he feared he would lose control of himself, for instance by having fainting spells. That is, his unconscious threatened to overcome him. He feared his persona, the mask he wore, would crack, and he would no longer be able to fool himself. He would encounter a big emptiness. The fears and weaknesses, his repressed complexes, would surface and he would be exposed.

The various symptoms threatened the inflated ego, which Ehud went to great efforts to sustain. He was afraid of "the group" that, like the chorus in Greek drama, commented on the play of his persona. The essence of weakness and mortality was forcefully suppressed, constellating as an ominous autonomous complex rather than linking ego to Self, which is the task of the constructive complex.

Integration of the Complex

Ehud's unconscious was no less stubborn than his conscious ego, and finally forced him to confront his shadow. He developed obsessive fears that beggars lay in wait for him outside his house, demanding he share his wealth. In one dream he drives along a highway, but decides to get off the road "in order to make a short-cut." He ends up in a dead end—an appropriately depressing image for where he had arrived in his life—in which dirty needles are spread around on the ground, making it difficult to walk. One cannot but recall Freud's dream of Irma, in which his patient is injected with a syringe that "probably . . . was not clean."[299] There can be no healing of the soul without the introduction of the shadow.

Or, in another dream, Ehud falls into a sewer, getting all dirty, embarrassed even to enter a nearby shop to buy soap and clean "at least my face"; that is, he can no longer easily restore his persona.

By means of these and other dreams, Ehud's unconscious labored to make him reconnect with the repressed complexes. The dreams were compensatory to his one-sided and inflated consciousness, and strived to establish appropriate equilibrium between Self and ego. This entails coming to terms with the reality that everything personal is wounded, crippled and mortal, in contrast to the archetypal. This is, I believe, the essence of Oedipus' solution to the Sphinx's riddle, sending her back, at least momentarily, to the realm of the unconscious where she belongs.

Jung says, "Recognition of the shadow . . . leads to the modesty we

---

[299] *The Interpretation of Dreams,* SE 4, pp. 106ff.

need in order to acknowledge imperfection."[300] Our complexes are our wounds, and if we are defensive or unconscious about them, they cripple us. To become aware of a crippling complex is, inevitably, part of the healing process.

Well into therapy, Ehud had the following dream:

> I feel as if I'm a cripple—as if I can't walk. I feel it is only a game, I am pretending, and I don't take it seriously. I try to go different places, and it looks quite funny. I kind of try to see what it feels like. Then I am getting more and more interested, and I want to understand it better, what it is all about. But then suddenly I fall and to my surprise I don't manage to get up on my feet. I am not sure if I really can't or if it is part of a game. This happens outside a small house, almost like a hut. Inside the hut is an old man, who tells me I have no right yet to come any closer.

To be crippled is to carry one's shadow. Here the dream-ego just pretends to be crippled, it is "as if" crippled. The game-playing itself, pretension, prevents true relatedness and inward authenticity; it disconnects Ehud's ego from the inner authority of the Self.

Ehud is not really pretending to be crippled. Rather, it is the other way around—pretension is his crippledness. The falseness and pretension constitute the disease; the crippling shadow complex that the ego drags along and that weakens the ego makes it fall. The symbolic dream image has fused the pathology—the meaning of pretension as inauthenticity toward Ehud himself—with its crippling expression and resulting weakness, the inability to stand up. The ego can only integrate its crippledness, the falseness, by feeling and understanding, by Eros and Logos.

In the dream Ehud goes to a small house, or hut, possibly a better self-representation than the big houses he preferred in external reality. Inside the hut resides the old man's wisdom. However, Ehud must not be arrogant. He has not yet gained the right to enter. At this stage, it would be dangerous, since he might rush in, make the hut into a fashionable house, and perhaps slay the old man! In contrast to his usual ego-in-hubris, he now had to recognize the truth of his crippledness, humbly and patiently enduring the suffering.

While complexes approaching consciousness often appear in dreams as something to be let in, for instance a stranger knocking on the door or an

---

[300] "The Undiscovered Self," *Civilization in Transition,* CW 10, par. 579

animal that has to be brought home to be cared for, there are places the ego must not go without paying due respect. Oedipus, even as an old man who makes his way "by aid of borrowed eyes," must "not walk in the silent dell, there, where the water and the honey-draught are poured." The elders of Colonus tell him, "Poor wanderer, if you have anything to say, leave the forbidden ground, and speak where speech is lawful, or else be silent."[301] That is, there are places in the soul that should not be rushed into, and dream images that should not be interpreted too hastily.

With Ehud, the quality of the transference now changed considerably. There was less need for him to have his persona reflected in the therapist's mirror. He seemed to want less ego-assurance, and coped better with the frustration of not receiving much narcissistic gratification. He could see the reason for the therapist's support of his shadow, and realize the role of weakness on the road to wholeness. This set off a whole new series of dreams, in which he had to care for a small boy. While the initial dreams of this cycle dealt with his having forgotten a baby boy, or exposed him to danger, he would later find himself "called back home" to care for the child. As his general attitude changed, he dreamed of entering a small house where he found an old man with a little child in his lap. As the child stood up, he could no longer tell its age, but it was limping. This marked a growing capacity to accept his own crippledness and imperfection.

The healing of pathology caused by the autonomy of the complex takes place initially by searching for and finding it, for example by free or focused association. A major purpose of associations is to "moisten the mind," to loosen it up, to "step out of the ego."

At the end of *Oedipus the King,* trying to resolve the epidemic that has struck Thebes, Oedipus asks, "Where shall we hope to uncover the faded traces of that far-distant crime?" to which Creon answers, "Here—the god said. Seek, and ye shall find. Unsought goes undetected."[302]

That is to say, complexes are often nearby, in the "neighborhood" or just around the corner (as Simpleton's feather knew), but they have to be looked for. That means the complex has to be consciously related to. Both Eros, relating, and Logos, interpretation, are involved. While the primary, teleological task of the complex is to dismember the archetype in order to enable its assimilation into the conscious personality, the split-off autono-

---

[301] Sophocles, *Oedipus at Colonus,* in *The Theban Plays,* p. 76.
[302] Ibid., p. 28.

mous complex needs to be re-membered. This does not only mean to re-member actual events, which would rely primarily on the notion of external traumata. For instance, an unconscious father complex may surface, as in one patient's dream in which she visits her late father in his small shop. She finds him confused, "in need to be brought home and cared for."

Resolving autonomous complexes is what we regularly do, technically not different from other schools of therapy and analysis, since it concerns bringing them into consciousness. In a significant passage, Jung states,

> Feeling-toned complexes in the unconscious do not change in the same way that they do in consciousness. Although they may be enriched by associations, they are not corrected . . . they take on the uninfluenceable and compulsive character of an automatism, of which they can be divested only if they are made conscious. This later procedure is rightly regarded as one of the most important therapeutic factors.[303]

In consciousness, says Jung, the complexes lose their automatic character and can therefore be corrected:

> They slough off their mythological envelope, and by entering into the adaptive process going forward in consciousness, they personalize and rationalize themselves [so that] a dialectical discussion becomes possible.[304]

That is, a change in conscious attitude reduces the automatic or compulsive character of the autonomous complex, transforming it into a complex that can fulfil its task of linking the archetypal and mythological with the personal ego.

Free association constitutes an Eros of the mind; it softens the ego and relaxes its boundaries. It is therefore essential for the freeing up of consciousness, enabling the ego to move toward the realm of images, fantasies and creativity. "Symbols are used to work out complexes," says Verena Kast.[305] The compulsive character of autonomous complexes is antithetical to symbolization, and in complexes caused by extreme trauma we find severe impairment in symbol-formation.

Eros puts the ego in touch with the complex, even if the latter has taken the shape of, as one analysand said, "a dwarf with a distorted face that I

---

[303] "On the Nature of the Psyche," *The Structure and Dynamics of the Psyche,* CW 8, par. 383.
[304] Ibid., par. 384.
[305] *The Dynamics of Symbols,* p. 40.

have to pull out of the garbage." It creates a real feeling between ego and complex rather than having the feeling-tone of the autonomous complex remain split-off from consciousness.

Logos, interpretation, brings the energy of the complex into the ego. A neurotic young man, afraid of his own sexuality, having lowered "the volume of his libido" in real life, dreams that he travels by New York underground. Next to him sits a young black man, singing and drumming to the loud music that pours out of his tape-recorder. The dreamer is very annoyed, but finds no escape as the black man introduces himself as Mr. Schwartz (that is, Black, a common Jewish name). The dream symbol has ingeniously combined the dream-ego with his black shadow, in need of integration. The dreamer did not realize this himself, but needed the interpretation in order to admit the dream image into consciousness.

Sometimes, however, the Logos-part may be superfluous. A fifty-year-old woman dreams of a three-eyed baby being born from the mosaic that is uncovered as she washes layers of dust off the floor, by hard labor on her knees. This may be the birth, out of newly uncovered motherly feelings, of the inward looking eye, more soulful than her usually very rational and reality-oriented outlook. But interpretation kills, and such an interpretation might have put back the dust of too much Logos, before the complex image could be integrated into consciousness. Thus, the remembering of complexes derives only partly, not solely, from cognition.

Castration at the Gateway to Individuation

When complexes become appropriately assimilated and integrated into the ego, the dialogue between ego and the unconscious opens up and the movement becomes freer and less obstructed. The integration of complexes enables openness toward the not-I, and the prospects of a dynamic and vital ego-Self relationship, rather than avoidance, splitting and compulsion. Integration of complexes is, thus, essential to the individuation process.

In the Oedipus myth incest has taken place concretely, signifying an undifferentiated union between the complex and the feminine aspect of the ego. At the end of *Oedipus the King,* realizing his terrible fate, Oedipus stabs out his eyes. When the limited vision of empirical eyes—"ego-vision"—ends, the complex's rule over the kingdom of the ego terminates. As Edinger says, "When Oedipus can see physically, he is blind psychologically; and as he comes to see psychologically, he becomes blind physically."[306]

In André Gide's version, Oedipus cannot accept happiness based on falsehood, and therefore destroys it.[307] Oedipus speaks thus:

> Ever since my own body's eyes through my own hand took away the world of appearance, I think I have actually begun to see. Yes: while the outer world covered for ever my body's eyes, it opened in me a new line of sight toward the unending perspective of an inner world which I had scorned to that point because only the world of appearance existed for me. And this world which is incomprehensible to our senses is the only true world which I now know. All else is simply an illusion which deludes us and confuses our contemplation of the divine. "One must stop seeing the world to gaze upon god," the blind prophet Teiresias said to me one day; and at that time I did not understand him, as you yourself, Theseus, do not understand me. I am conscious of that.[308]

This reflects castration of the ego complex and conscious identity, which often is considered to be the end of the story. However, after his long wanderings, Oedipus becomes a holy man, and later his tomb blesses the land it is on. Thus, his Self came to transcend his individual destiny.

It pertains to the wisdom of the crone and the old man that complexes no longer serve as the path whereupon the archetypal energies can be animated and transform into human shape. Rather, as the ego renounces its unmitigated vantage point, the complexes come to serve, in Jung's words, as "other luminaries besides the sun [the ego]," from which "an observation of the ego complex from another standpoint somewhere in the same psyche is equally possible."[309]

This, however, brings us from *Oedipus the King* to *Oedipus at Colonus*, away from the complex, toward the world of archetypes, to the boundary between man and destiny, death and growth.

---

[306] *The Eternal Drama*, p. 130. See also *The Psyche on Stage*, pp. 81ff.

[307] See Helen Watson-Williams, *André Gide and the Greek Myth*, pp. 115, 163.

[308] Kerényi, "Oedipus: Two Essays," in Kerényi and Hillman, *Odeipus Variations*, p. 71.

[309] *Mysterium Coniunctionis*, CW 14, par. 502.

Bibliography

Adler, Gerhard. *Studies in Analytical Psychology.* New York: G. P. Putnam's Sons, 1966.

Andersen, Hans Christian. *The Complete Illustrated Works.* London: Chancellor Press, 1996.

Apollodorus. *Apollodorus: The Library.* Trans. James G. Frazer. 2 vols. Cambridge, MA: Harvard University Press, 1992.

Beebe, John. "Attitudes toward the Unconscious." In *Journal of Analytical Psychology,* vol. 42 (1997).

Bettelheim, Bruno. *The Children of the Dream.* Frogmore: Paladin, 1971.

Bischof, Ledford J. *Interpreting Personality Theories.* New York: Harper and Row, 1964.

Brod, Max. *Franz Kafka: A Biography.* New York: Da Capo Press, 1995.

Campbell, Joseph. *The Hero with a Thousand Faces.* New York: Bollingen, 1968.

Carotenuto, Aldo. *A Secret Symmetry: Sabina Spielrein between Jung and Freud.* New York: Pantheon Books, 1982.

Cooper, J.C. *An Illustrated Encyclopaedia of Traditional Symbols.* London: Thames and Hudson, 1987.

Dieckmann, Hans. *Complexes: Diagnosis and Therapy in Analytical Psychology.* Trans. Boris Matthews. Wilmette, IL: Chiron Publications, 1999.

Donn, Linda. *Freud and Jung: Years of Friendship, Years of Loss.* New York: Scribner, 1988.

Edinger, E. F. *The Bible and the Psyche: Individuation Symbolism in the Old Testament.* Toronto: Inner City Books, 1986.

_____. *The Creation of Consciousness: Jung's Myth for Modern Man.* Toronto: Inner City Books, 1984.

_____. *Ego and Archetype: Individuation and the Religious Function of the Psyche.* New York: Penguin, 1973.

_____. *The Eternal Drama: The Inner Meaning of Greek Mythology.* Boston: Shambhala, 1994.

_____. *The Psyche on Stage: Individuation Motifs in Shakespeare and Sophocles.* Toronto: Inner City Books, 2000.

Elder, George R. *The Body (An Encyclopedia of Archetypal Symbolism, Vol. 2).* Boston: Shambhala, 1996.

Eliot, Alexander. *The Universal Myths: Heroes, Gods, Tricksters and Others.* New York: Meridian, 1990.

Ellenberger, Henri F. *The Discovery of the Unconscious.* New York: Basic Books, 1970.

Everest, Pauline. "The Multiple Self: Working with Dissociation and Trauma." In *Journal of Analytical Psychology*, vol. 44 (1999).

Fordham, Frieda. *An Introduction to Jung's Psychology.* Harmondsworth: Penguin, 1973.

Freud, Sigmund. *Standard Edition of the Complete Psychological Works.* 24 vols. London: The Hogarth Press, 1953-1973.

Frey-Rohn, Liliane. *From Freud to Jung: A Comparative Study of the Unconscious.* Boston: Shambhala, 1990.

Glatzer, Nahum, ed. *Franz Kafka: The Complete Stories.* New York: Schocken, 1995.

Grimm Brothers. *The Complete Grimm's Fairy Tales.* New York: Pantheon Books, 1972.

———— . *Grimm's Grimmsar.* San Francisco: Chronicle Books, 1997.

Harding, M. Esther. *Woman's Mysteries: Ancient and Modern.* Boston: Shambhala, 1990.

Hillman, James. "On the Necessity of Abnormal Psychology: Ananke and Athene." In James Hillman, ed., *Facing the Gods.* Dallas: Spring Publications, 1980.

Hitler, Adolph. *Mein Kampf.* Boston: Houghton Mifflin, 1943.

Jacobi, Jolande. *Complex/Archetype/Symbol.* New York: Bollingen, 1971.

Jaffé, Aniela, ed. *C.G. Jung: Word and Image* (Bollingen Series XCVII:2). Princeton: Princeton University Press, 1979.

Jones, Ernest. *Sigmund Freud: Life and Work.* London: Hogarth Press, 1955.

Jung, C.G. *The Collected Works* (Bollingen Series XX). 20 vols. Trans. R.F.C. Hull. Ed. H. Read, M. Fordham, G. Adler, Wm. McGuire. Princeton: Princeton University Press, 1953-1979.

———— . *Memories, Dreams, Reflections.* Ed. Aniela Jaffé. New York: Vintage, 1965.

Kafka, Franz. *Letter to Father.* Trans. Karen Reppin. Prague: Vitalis, 1999.

———— . *Letters to Friends, Family and Editors.* Trans. Richard and Clara Winston. London: Calder, 1978.

Kast, Verena. *The Dynamics of Symbols.* New York: Fromm International 1992

Ka-Tzetnik. *Shivitti*. San Francisco: Harper and Row, 1989.

Kerényi, Karl, and Hillman, James. *Oedipus Variations:Studies]in Literature and Psychoanalysis*. Dallas: Spring, 1995.

Kerr, John. *A Most Dangerous Method*. New York: Knopf, 1993.

Kirsch, Thomas. *The Jungians: A Comparative and Historical Perspective*. Philadelphia: Routledge, 2000.

Knafo, Danielle. "The Significance of the Oedipal in Dreams of Freud and Jung." In *The International Review of Psycho-Analysis*, vol. 19 (1992).

Lao Tsu. *Tao-te Ching*. Trans. Gia-fu Feng and Jane English. New York: Viking Books, 1972.

Laplanche, J., and Pontalis, J.B. *The Language of Psychoanalysis*. London: Karnac, 1988.

Levinson, D. *The Seasons of a Man's Life*. New York: Ballantine Books, 1978.

Mairowitz, David Z., and Crumb, R. *Introducing Kafka*. New York: Totem, 1993.

McGuire, Wm. *The Freud/Jung Letters* (Bollingen Series XCIV). Trans. Ralph Manheim and R.F.C. Hull. New York: Penguin, 1979.

_____. "Jung's Complex Reactions (1907): Word Association Experiments Performed by Binswanger." In *Spring 1984*.

McGuire, Wm., and Hull, R.F.C., eds. *C.G. Jung Speaking* (Bollingen Series XCVII). Princeton: Princeton University Press, 1977.

Neumann, Erich. *Amor and Psyche*. Princeton: Princeton University Press, 1973.

_____. *The Fear of the Feminine*. Princeton: Princeton University Press, 1994.

_____. *The Great Mother*. London: Routledge and Kegan Paul, 1963.

_____. *The Origins and History of Consciousness*. Princeton: Princeton University Press, 1970.

Roazen, Paul. *Freud and His Followers*. Hamondsworth, UK: Peregrine, 1979.

Ryce-Menuhin, Joel. *Jung and the Monotheisms*. New York: Routledge, 1994.

Samuels, Andrew. *Jung and the Post-Jungians*. London: Routledge and Kegan Paul, 1985.

_____, ed. *The Father: Contemporary Jungian Perspectives*. New York University Press, 1986.

Samuels, Andrew; Shorter, Bani; and Plaut, Fred, eds. *A Critical Dictionary of Jungian Analysis*. London: Routledge and Kegan Paul, 1986.

Satinover, Jeffrey. "Jung's Lost Contribution to the Dilemma of Narcissism." In *Journal of the American Psychoanalytic Association*, vol. 34 (1986).

Schärf Kluger, Rivkah. *Satan in the Old Testament.* Evanston, IL: Northwestern University Press, 1967.

Scholem, Gershom. *Major Trends in Jewish Mysticism.* New York: Schocken Books, 1961.

Shalit, Erel. *The Hero and His Shadow: Psychopolitical Aspects of Myth and Reality in Israel.* Lanham: University Press of America, 1999.

_____. "Shadows in Jerusalem: Beyond the Hill of Evil Counsel, Towards the Valley of Hell." Stockholm: Center for Jungian Psychology, 1998.

Sharp, Daryl. *Jung Lexicon: A Primer of Terms and Concepts.* Toronto: Inner City Books, 1991.

_____. *The Secret Raven: Conflict and Transformation in the Life of Franz Kafka.* Toronto: Inner City Books, 1980.

Sophocles. *The Theban Plays.* New York: Baltimore: Penguin Classics, 1974.

Spiro, Melford E. *Children of the Kibbutz.* New York: Schocken, 1965.

Stein, Robert. *Incest and Human Love.* Baltimore: Penguin, 1974.

Storr, Anthony. *Churchill's Black Dog.* London: HarperCollins, 1990.

von Franz, Marie-Louise. *Creation Myths.* Boston: Shambhala, 1995.

_____. *The Interpretation of Fairy Tales.* Dallas: Spring, 1987.

_____. "The Process of Individuation." In C.G. Jung, ed., *Man and His Symbols.* New York: Anchor, 1964.

Walker, Barbara. *The Woman's Encyclopaedia of Myths and Secrets.* San Francisco: HarperCollins, 1983.

Watson-Williams, Helen. *André Gide and the Greek Myth.* London: Oxford University Press, 1967.

Weisstub, Eli. "Self as the Feminine Principle." In *Journal of Analytical Psychology,* vol. 42 (1997).

Winnicott, D.W. *Collected Papers.* London: Tavistock, 1958.

_____. *Playing and Reality.* Harmondsworth, UK: Penguin, 1980.

Wolff, Toni. "Structural Forms of the Feminine Psyche." Monograph privately printed for the Students' Association. Zurich: C.G. Jung Institute, 1956.

_____. *Studien zu C.G. Jungs Psychologie.* Zurich: Rhein-Verlag, 1959.

Index